iCourse · 课程

大学英语应用类课程系列

跨文化交际与地球村民

主编　高永晨

编者　沈鞠明　张凤娟　郝吉环

*Intercultural Communication
—What Global Villagers Have to Know*

高等教育出版社·北京

图书在版编目（CIP）数据

跨文化交际与地球村民 ：汉、英 ／ 高永晨主编 . --
北京 ：高等教育出版社，2017.3（2025.1重印）

iCourse·教材

ISBN 978-7-04-046989-9

Ⅰ．①跨… Ⅱ．①高… Ⅲ．①文化交流－英语－高等
学校－教材 Ⅳ．①G115

中国版本图书馆CIP数据核字 (2017) 第000673 号

策划编辑　谢　森　　责任编辑　谢　森　马小洁　　封面设计　张　志　　版式设计　孙　伟
责任校对　巩　熠　　责任印制　刁　毅

出版发行	高等教育出版社		网　　址	http://www.hep.edu.cn
社　　址	北京市西城区德外大街4号			http://www.hep.com.cn
邮政编码	100120		网上订购	http://www.hepmall.com.cn
印　　刷	河北鹏远艺兴科技有限公司			http://www.hepmall.com
开　　本	850mm×1168mm　1/16			http://www.hepmall.cn
印　　张	14.75			
字　　数	361千字		版　　次	2017年3月第1版
购书热线	010-58581118		印　　次	2025年1月第9次印刷
咨询电话	400-810-0598		定　　价	38.00元

本书如有缺页、倒页、脱页等质量问题，请到所购图书销售部门联系调换

版权所有　侵权必究

物料号　46989-00

总　序

　　进入21世纪，我国的教育发展和国际交流对大学生应用英语从事跨文化交际活动和解决实际问题的能力提出了更高的要求。苏州大学的大学外语教学团队在反思传统教学经验的基础上，深入研究国内外外语教学前沿理论和成果，理论联系课堂一线教学实际，积极展开英语教学改革的实践，于2003年建设了由"英语高级口语""英语写作与翻译""英语报刊选读""影视英语""跨文化交际""中国地方文化英语教学"六门课组成的"大学英语应用类课程"。五年内，有数千名学生选修了这些课程，实际教学效果甚好。该系列课程于2009年获得"国家精品课程"称号。

　　近年来，我国信息技术高速发展，一个全新的外语教学模式正在形成。为了满足当代大学生对"互联网+"条件下的学习需求，我们依托教育部的"爱课程"网站，进一步完善了对国家精品课程——"大学英语应用类课程"的建设，从教学重点和难点、知识点和能力点、教学录像和教学课件等多方面大大完善了该课程体系的数字化资源的配套建设，为更多的在校大学生和社会英语学习爱好者提供了优质、方便的网络学习资源，更好地履行了高校服务社会的职责。由于"大学英语应用类课程"的优质共享资源建设成果突出，产生了积极的社会影响，于2016年荣获教育部第一批"国家精品资源共享课"称号。

　　教育部大学外语教学指导委员会最新研制的《大学英语教学指南（送审稿）》指出大学英语的教学目标是"培养学生的英语应用能力，增强跨文化交际意识和交际能力，同时发展自主学习能力，提高综合文化素养，使他们在学习、生活、社会交往和未来工作中能够有效地使用英语，满足国家、社会、学校和个人发展的需要"。为落实该《指南》精神，我们进一步反思了关于国家精品资源共享课程——"大学英语应用类课程"的建设问题。为积极推进大学英语教学与信息技术的深度融合，及时为学习者提供线上线下个性化、多样化、便捷化的"互联网+"学习条件，我们的课程团队专门组织编写并出版了与数字课程相配套的纸质教材，目前共涵盖5门课程的5本教材：《英语口语新教程：成功交流》《大学英语写作与翻译：生成及其转换》《英语影视欣赏》《跨文化交际与地球村民》以及《中国特色文化英语教程》。

　　该系列教材的编写理念充分体现了工具性与人文性统一的大学英语教学理念和目标，具有如下三方面的特色：

一、教材充分发挥"互联网+"信息技术优势，尤其是充分发挥移动互联网信息技术特长，电子教案、视频材料、二维码等呈现形式充分支持课堂内外、线上线下、微课、翻转课堂等多元教学方法、教学手段和教学环境的应用，有利于教师有效地实施混合式教学模式，促进学生主动学习能力和合作学习能力的发展。

二、教材题材和体裁广泛，课文取材既体现语言的经典性，又不乏时效性，所承载的信息既体现了全球化特色又突显了地方风格，尤其注重向世界传播中国地方文化精华和人文风貌。

三、教材的课文以及练习设计充分遵循外语学习科学规律，既注意满足当代大学生的学习生活兴趣，又力求激发和培养其创造性和批判性思维，并着力创造条件，促进学生进行语言输入、大脑机制内化到语言输出的循环运用实践，为学生从英语词汇到语块、英语单句到段落、篇章的多层次英语使用提供了充裕的实践机会。

　　总之，我们衷心希望这套依托教育部"爱课程网"的国家精品资源共享课"大学英语应用类课程"的课程教材能够突破我国传统外语学习在空间和时间上的限制，满足移动"互联网+"时代英语学习者的个性化需求，帮助其更大程度地获得英语学习和应用的成就感。

孙倚娜

2016年12月

前　言

　　随着经济全球化以及与之相伴随的文化全球化的狂飙猛进，无论是现实生活中的地理空间还是虚拟的网络空间，都使得麦克卢汉（Marshall McLuhan）于1962年提出的"地球村"（global village）概念变成了现实。生活在"地球村"里的每一个村民都或多或少地被卷进了一张连接全球不同民族、不同种族、不同肤色和不同语言文化的大网。然而，世界上不同的人们都分属于不同的社会制度、不同的地理环境和不同的宗教信仰，有着各具特色的民族传统，信奉不同的意识形态和价值观念，其生活方式，思维方式、交流方式、认知体系、规范体系、语言和非语言符号体系等都存在着显著的文化差异。在跨文化交际中出现因文化差异而造成的文化之间的隔膜、误解、矛盾乃至冲突时常发生。人们需要通过学习跨文化交际知识，了解不同文化背景，分析文化冲突根源，达到有效得体的跨文化交际目的。因此，培养跨文化交际能力对肩负着人类历史使命的年轻地球村民来说显得尤为重要和迫切。教育部高等学校外语教学指导委员会在新近研制的《大学英语教学指南》中，将课程设置分为"通用英语、专门用途英语、跨文化交际"（2015，王守仁）三个模块。这是我国首次把"跨文化交际"作为大学英语教学内容之一。可见，提高大学生跨文化交际能力已成为高等学校外语教育的当务之急。

　　《跨文化交际与地球村民》基于"知行合一"的跨文化交际模式，遵循循序渐进、与时俱进、学以致用的原则。通过对中西方文化异同的展示和分析，努力剖析其中蕴涵的深层文化根源，提供丰富的跨文化交际语境，引导学生发现问题之源，培养分析问题和解决问题的能力，增强多元文化意识，克服民族文化中心主义，提高跨文化交际能力。我们围绕主题，精心选择每一篇文章，用心设计每一个练习，并根据多年积累的跨文化交际教学的经验和使用本教材的体会，参考和整合了国内外最新素材，推出了这本与"爱课程"相匹配、供高等学校非英语专业本科学生使用的教材。

　　本教材由十个主题构成十个单元。前七个单元与"爱课程"上的七个讲课专题一一对应，依次是：全球化与跨文化交际、交际与文化、言语交际、非言语交际、文化价值观、文化休克和跨文化交际能力。从第八单元起的后三个单元是全新的内容，依次是：教育中的跨文化交际、商业中的跨文化交际、网络中的跨文化交际。整本教材各单元既独立成章，又前后贯通，环环紧扣，从理论到实践，无不体现出编者的用心良苦。每个单元由四个模块组成：Warm Up，Readings，Exercises，Additional Reading。我们从引出主题、导入主题内容，再到练习和拓展，力求从不同视角介绍和探讨跨文化交际的主要内容和一些重要问题，也给学有余力的学生对同一主题提供了进一步研修的阅读文献。每单元的练习又分为四个部分：Culture Quiz，Group Discussion，Intercultural Practice，Case Studies，内容丰富，趣味性、互动性、操作性均很强，可供学生课内外讨论或实践。希望通过这些环节的训练，促使学生主动把跨文化交际知识转化为有效得体的跨文化交际行为，真正做到知行合一，知行并进，行其所知，知其所行，全面提高自身的综合素养，在全球化时代做个合格的地球村民。

本教材是苏州大学国家精品课程教材中的一部。在此我们衷心感谢各级领导，尤其是外国语学院副院长孙倚娜教授给予我们的鼓励和支持，感谢高等教育出版社的领导和编辑的认真负责精神和热情帮助，感谢美籍教师Jia Ruo对本教材所做的详尽审阅。另外，还要感谢许多国内外专家学者为我们提供的宝贵参考书目。同时也要感谢本课题组的老师们，在完成国家社科基金项目的同时，马不停蹄地昼夜忙碌，才有了今天的收获。

由于受学识水平和条件的限制，教材中难免会存在一些缺憾，恳请读者提出宝贵意见，以便再版时进一步修订完善。教师用户如需参考答案，请在中国外语网（http://www.cflo.com.cn）下载。

编　者
2016年11月

Contents

Contents

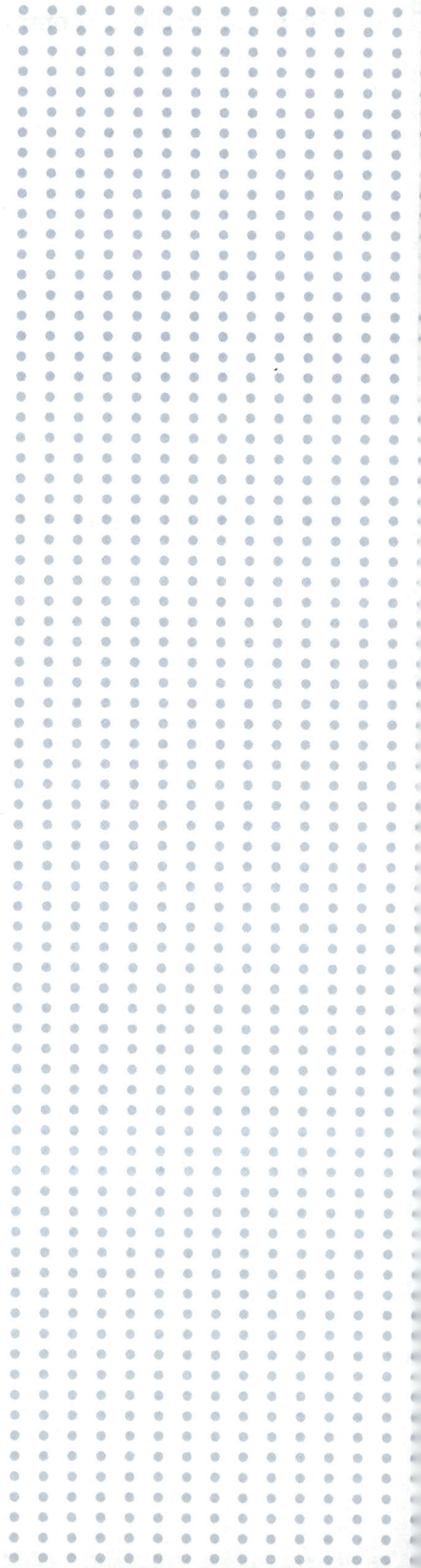

Globalization and Intercultural Communication

*Human beings draw close to one another by their
common nature, but habits and customs keep them
apart.*

— Confucius

We are alike and we are different.
— L. A. Samovar & R. E. Porter

*Our most basic common link is that we all inhabit
this planet.*

— John F. Kennedy

PART ❶ Warm Up

1. Watch a video clip about William's smile to get some idea about cultural differences.
2. Read the following dialogue about globalization and answer the questions below it.

A: What is the best definition of globalization?

B: Princess Diana's death.

A: How come?

B: An English princess with an Egyptian boyfriend crashes in a French tunnel, driving a German car with a Dutch engine, driven by a Belgian who was drunk on Scottish whisky, followed closely by Italian Paparazzi, on Japanese motorcycles; they are treated by an American doctor, using Brazilian medicine. And this is sent to you by a Canadian, using Bill Gates' "world flattening" technology, and you're probably reading this from a computer with a Taiwanese chip, and a Korean monitor, assembled by Bangladeshi workers in a Singaporean plant, transported by Indian lorry-drivers, hijacked by Indonesians, unloaded by Sicilian longshoremen, and trucked to you by undocumented Mexican immigrants...

That, my friend, is globalization!

Questions

1. What do you think of this definition of globalization?
2. How much do you know about globalization?
3. How much do you know about intercultural communication?
4. In the picture, can you figure out how many nationalities of the diners there are? Discuss what are the possibilities that brought them together?

PART ❷   Readings

Passage 1 ▶ What Is Globalization

Globalization can be described as a process by which the people of the world are unified into a single society and function together. This process is a combination of economic, technological, socio-cultural and political forces. Globalization is often used to refer to economic globalization, that is, integration of national economies into the international economy through trade, foreign direct investment, capital flows, migration, and the spread of technology.

When we talk about global business, we mean that the money and products of different regions and countries are becoming more interdependent and interrelated. When we talk about global politics we mean that different countries make decisions as parts of a large world community rather than as completely autonomous[①] entities.

The beginning of the modern globalization era is usually marked in 1989 with the end of the Cold War era. However, as Friedman points out, the actual trend toward globalization has been running since the mid-1800s:

> The first era of globalization and global finance capitalism [from the mid-1800s to the late 1920s] was broken apart by the successive hammer blows of World War I, the Russian Revolution and the Great Depression, which combined to fracture[②] the world both physically and ideologically. The formally divided world that emerged after World War II was then frozen in place by the Cold War... It lasted roughly from 1945 to 1989, when, with the fall of the Berlin Wall, it was replaced by another system: the era of globalization we are now in.

Globalization has many causes including improved technology, social trends, and economic development. But globalism isn't just a historical inevitability; in many respects, globalism has become a politically driven force. After World War II, leaders around the world began to recognize the urgent need for greater cooperation between governments and economies.

Notes
① 独立的
② 使···破碎

Notes
③ 责任
④ 关税及贸易总协定
（1947 年签订）
⑤ 驯化的
⑥ 必须履行的责任

To increase cooperation and mutual accountability③ , several political and economic institutions were founded, including: the United Nations (UN), the International Monetary Fund (IMF), the World Bank, the General Agreement on Tariffs and Trade (GATT④).

Today, although some critics argue that these institutions have come to be a domesticating⑤ force for weaker nations, most still feel uneasy about nations that are not acting as healthy members of the global community. Nations are urged (and even forced) to maintain open political processes, adhere to internationally accepted legal norms, and extend open markets and market information. So globalization is not just a trend, it's an imperative⑥ .

(Adapted from "Globalization and Communication" by John Jamison)

Questions

1. Do you prefer the definition of globalization given in the passage? Why or why not?
2. Why is globalization often used to refer to economic globalization?
3. How do you understand "globalization is not just a trend, it's an imperative?"

Passage 2 ▶ Thinking Globally

Notes
① 麦克卢汉（1911–1980），世界著名的加拿大传播学家，1962 年在其著作 *Understanding Media: The Extension of Man* 中首次提出了"地球村"这个术语

In 1962, the Canadian writer Marshall McLuhan① introduced the term "global village" to express the idea that the world seems to be getting smaller. The planet Earth is not shrinking, but time and space are.

In a village, residents communicate with other residents face to face. They usually meet formally from time to time to share information and make decisions, but most of the time information and opinions flow from person to person informally in talks between neighbors and family members. They know when other residents have suffered a disaster or are celebrating good fortune. They help one another, quarrel, work together and against one another as feelings and circumstances require them to do so. They share each other's lives for better or for worse②. Now the whole world is like a village.

Trains, planes, telephones, televisions, the Internet, and other forms of modern transportation and communication reduce the time and distance that once kept the peoples of the world apart. Even people who do not travel far from home live in the global village. People who live in small towns watch television reports of wars and disasters half a world away and work in factories making goods for export to distant markets. Now a Chinese leader can meet with American students and journalists in a contemporary version of the village meeting, and the rest of the world will listen in by means of a television signal carried by a satellite orbiting the earth.

In the metaphor③ of the global village, nations are like families and continents are like neighborhoods. People feel most at home in their own families, but they go out of the house regularly to do some business and to buy what they need in the market. Now markets and business are global. If a neighbor's house burns down, it affects everyone. Others may be expected to give shelter to the victims. The smoke and flames may threaten someone else's home and family. If someone dumps garbage into the village well, the neighbors can't say it is his own business, because they also get their water from that well.

Residents want to stay on good terms with their neighbors. They may simply think that is the proper and civilized way to live. They may consider their neighbors to be a lot like them and therefore understand them and like them. They may remember that some neighbors helped them when they had some trouble. Perhaps they have just learned that life is better when people cooperate with one another. If some residents of the village have had trouble with their neighbors in the past or think they are strange or inferior, they may be suspicious and on guard to protect themselves from harm in the future.

As in a village the nations (families) of the world are dependent on one another. Time and space no longer isolate or protect nations and groups from each other. As global environmental problems become more serious, people realize that the rivers of the world flow and the winds of the planet blow without regard to national boundaries. The economic, political and military actions of other nations are the actions of our neighbors. We might wish that we could treat them as distant events that do not concern us, but in the global village that is no longer possible.

Notes
② 不论怎样
③ 隐喻

Notes
④ 后殖民的

Not everyone welcomes this image of the global village. To some it seems like an image of post-colonial ④ dominance of the world by the West. They prefer to see the world in terms of their own family or their own nation. They may say, "We do not want to live in a village that someone else makes for us and controls." They worry that the global economy will have everyone resemble the families of the world that have the most economic and political power. They do not want to be second-class citizens in this village, and they do not want to give up their own treasured ways of life.

Others worry that conflict will increase as time and distance shrink. From news reports everyone can see that religious, ethnic, economic, and political differences continue to divide people. They rightly ask, "How can I and the members of my family get along with members of that other family who seem so different from us?" They see troubles in other families and wonder why they can't solve their problems. Above all, every family wants to protect itself. No one wants the problems of another family to spread to their family.

Whatever anxiety people have about the global village, they can see that contact among the peoples of the world is increasing. If the world is becoming more like a village, as its residents we want it to be a place we feel comfortable living in. Everyone wants to benefit from global trade and advanced technology, and they want to live among people who respect and appreciate one another. They want to protect themselves from danger and live at peace with their neighbors. But most people do not want peace imposed on them by the power of another family. They want to live as they have chosen to.

These are some of the challenges of living in a global village. To meet those challenges people everywhere need to learn about other cultures. They need to know their neighbors. They need to do more than know about them. They need to know how to get along with them and how to solve problems that inevitably arise. To do this it is necessary to learn how to communicate across cultures. That means global villagers need to learn to think, feel and behave in new ways. The reality of the global village challenges all its residents to develop a broader worldview, a more global psychology, and the cultural skills necessary for building relationships and solving problems across cultures.

(Adapted from "Doing Culture: Cross-Cultural Communication in Action"
by Linell Davis)

Questions

1. How do you understand the statement "the planet Earth is not shrinking, but time and space are?"
2. Why is it not his or her own business if someone dumps garbage into the village well? What do you think the author refers to by offering this vivid example?
3. Why do some people not welcome the image of the global village?
4. What are some of the challenges of living in a global village? And how to meet those challenges?

Passage 3 ▶ What Is Intercultural Communication

As the term suggests, intercultural communication occurs when a member of one culture produces a message for consumption by a member of another culture. In other words, intercultural communication is the communication between people from different cultural backgrounds. What happened on the Silk Road, Marco Polo's stay in China, Monk Jianzhen's mission to Japan, and Zheng He's seven voyages to the Western Seas all embody this idea. As a phenomenon, intercultural communication is as old as humankind, but as a discipline, its history is quite short.

Intercultural communication as a field of study first emerged in the United States in the 1950s as a result of the four trends that led to the development of the global village:

1) Convenient Transportation Systems:

In the form of transportation and communication systems, new technology has accelerated intercultural contact. Trips once taking days, weeks, or even months are now measured in hours. Transcontinental aviation[①] now makes it possible for tourists, business executives, or government officials to enjoy breakfast in San Francisco and dinner in Paris on the same day.

Notes
① 航空

Notes
② 隶属机构
③ 由同类部分组成的
④ 遗产
⑤ 无比的

2) Innovative Communication Systems:

Innovative communication systems have also encouraged and facilitated cultural interaction. Communication satellites, sophisticated television transmission equipment, and digital switching networks now allow people throughout the world to share information and ideas instantaneously.

3) Economic Globalization:

As we enter the 21st century, the United States is no longer the dominant economic force in the world. For example, according to Harris and Moran, there are now more than 37,000 transnational corporations with 207,000 foreign affiliates ② . This expansion in globalization has resulted in multinational corporations participating in various international business arrangements such as joint ventures and licensing agreements. These and countless other economic ties mean that it would not be unusual for someone to work for an organization that does business in many countries.

4) Widespread Migrations:

In the United States, people are now redefining and rethinking the meaning of the word American. It can no longer be used to describe a somewhat homogeneous ③ group of people sharing a European heritage ④ . As Ben J. Wattenberg tells us, America has become the first universal nation, a truly multi-cultural society marked by unparalleled ⑤ diversity.

Today an Internet search on the topic of intercultural communication or cross-cultural communication yields over 100,000 results. In recent years practitioners in a wide variety of fields of scientific cooperation, academic research, business, management, education, health, culture, politics, diplomacy, development, and others have realized just how important intercultural communication is for their everyday work. Fast travel, international media, and the Internet have made it easy for us to communicate with people all over the world. The process of economic globalization means that we cannot function in isolation but must interact with the rest of the world for survival. The global nature of many widely diverse modern problems and issues such as the environment, governance of the Internet, poverty and international terrorism calls for cooperation between nations. Intercultural communication is no longer an option, but a necessity.

(Adapted from "Intercultural Communication: A Reader" by L. A. Samovar & R. E. Porter)

Questions

1. Why is intercultural communication as old as humankind?
2. What caused the development of the global village?
3. How do you understand the sentence "intercultural communication is no longer an option, but a necessity?"

PART ❸   Exercises

Section A▶ Culture Quiz

Watch the video *Globalization* and fill in the following blanks accordingly.

1. In today's world, economic, environmental, social and political issues and problems are no longer limited to _____, because the world becomes so interdependent.

2. Today, modern communication technology and mass media, like radio, TV, phones or the Internet, are _____. This means the information can be distributed worldwide in real time and for all the people.

3. Many companies are searching for new markets and opportunities for _____ in countries of low wages. The number of multinational corporations has risen from 7,000 to 65,000 since the 1990s.

4. Similar to the world economy, international politics are also more interdependent today. Most important policy issues like climate change, _____ or terrorism do not care about orders. Such problems cannot be solved by a single state alone.

5. The influence of globalization can be observed on cultures as well. Western culture, especially _____, becomes dominant and destroys the cultural diversity. A global distribution of Western music, news, products, or even the English language is a good case in point.

6. It becomes clear that globalization takes place in many areas such as economy, politics

and culture. Some countries benefit much from it while others benefit less. Thus globalization presents both _____ and _____.

Section B ▶ Group Discussion

Please discuss the following questions within your group. You can refer to any resource related to the questions if necessary.

1. What benefits and problems do you expect from life in the global village?
2. What's the relationship between globalization and intercultural communication?
3. Why should we learn intercultural communication?

Section C ▶ Intercultural Practice

Read the following passage first to get some idea about new changes in communication technology and political structures in recent decades. And then use the list of some developments and environmental issues to convince people that the world is becoming a global village and describe how each development or issue influences their life.

The 20th century witnessed great changes in communication technology. International communication that only a few decades ago took days, if not weeks, now takes seconds. With e-mail, faxes, the Internet, satellites, and telephones we can contact our international partners at a moment's notice. If we want a more personal exchange, teleconferencing is almost like bringing the other person right into our office. And if we want a true face-to-face discussion, jets can take us anywhere within hours. The variety of channels of communication is truly amazing. The choice of which channel to use in a particular situation is influenced by cultural priorities and values.

The changes in technology have facilitated the exchange of ideas, but they also have amplified the possibilities for cultural misunderstanding. It is so easy to assume that the person on the other end of the line (or e-mail or cell phone connection) communicates just as we do. After all, he or she uses the same technology and maybe even the same business terminology.

In addition to changes in technology, there have been massive political and economic changes in recent decades that affect business communication internationally. China is adopting a market-oriented economy with its own unique characteristics; India is embracing Web and cell phone communication. Small industrialized countries resent being bullied by big ones. Non-Western countries are becoming more assertive and protective of their cultural values and behaviors and do not accept Western business practices quietly any longer. In recent years the activity of international terrorists has generated increased vigilance around the world; Internet viruses are also a present threat to global communication channels.

As a result, understanding other cultures is more important than ever. If we consider that people with the same economic, political, and cultural background have problems communicating effectively, we can appreciate the difficulties and challenges that people from diverse cultures face when trying to communicate. Misunderstandings will always be a part of intercultural communication. But they can be minimized through an awareness of the priorities and expectations of the business partners.

(Adapted from "Intercultural Communication in the Global Workplace" by Iris Varner &
Linda Beamer)

Here are some developments and environmental issues for your reference:

1. Satellite transmission of telephone, radio and television signals;
2. International computer networks such as the Internet;
3. Increased speed and availability of air travel;
4. International economic relationships such as multi-national corporations and foreign trade;
5. Economic cooperation through organizations such as the European Union, the Association of Southeast Asian Nations, Asia-Pacific Economic Cooperation, and Asian Infrastructure Investment Bank;
6. Economic regulation through global organizations such as the World Trade Organization;
7. The movement of people from rural areas to cities and from developing countries to developed ones;
8. More intense political, military, and diplomatic relationships among nations;
9. Higher standards of living that give more people the chance to travel and enjoy their leisure, thus stimulating the growth of the international tourism industry;
10. Environmental issues such as over-fishing of the oceans, over-use of pesticide, global warming, deforestation, desertification, smog, endangered species of plants and animals, waste disposal, and air and water pollution.

Section D Case Studies

Case 1

Finding an Interested Buyer

George Gorski was excited to be in the People's Republic of China. This was his first visit, and he was interested in learning more about the culture and in making several contacts at the trade show. The opportunity to do business in China seemed like a real possibility. George had been very successful in his business deals in the United States and he prided himself on his ability to "get things moving."

His first day at the trade show in Beijing had gone well. He was able to look around at the various displays of sporting equipment and get some idea of who he might approach. He was sure his products, tennis racquets with an unusual new design, would raise some eyebrows. On the second day he approached the company that he felt would be most responsive to his products and introduced himself to the general manager, Mr. Li. Since he had read that the Chinese find getting down to business immediately too abrupt and rude, he began a casual conversation, eventually leading up to the topic of his products and suggesting how Mr. Li's company might benefit from using them. George then suggested that he arrange to get together with Mr. Li and provide more specifics and documentation on his products.

Mr. Li responded in fairly good English, "That would be interesting."

George felt a tremor of excitement as his mind reviewed the possibilities. Knowing that he had only a few days left in Beijing, George wanted to nail down a time. "When can we meet?" asked George.

"Ah. This week is very busy," replied Mr. Li.

"It sure is," said George. "How about tomorrow morning?"

"Tomorrow?" queried Mr. Li. "If I have time, it would be good."

"It will only take about half an hour. How about ten o'clock? Meet you here."

"Tomorrow at ten o'clock?" asked Mr. Li, thoughtfully.

"Right," George said, "I'll see you then?"

"Hmm, yes. Why don't you come by tomorrow?"

"Okay," George responded, "It was nice meeting you."

George was anxious to see what would happen with Mr. Li. As ten o'clock rolled around, he approached Mr. Li's company's exhibit only to find that Mr. Li had some important business and was not able to meet with him. George called later that day and was told that

Mr. Li was not available. Frustrated, George returned to his room for the evening.

(Adapted from "Turning Bricks into Jade" by Mary Margaret Wang et al.)

Which of the following might be the best culturally-based explanation for this incident?

A. Mr. Li had very important business matters to attend to and was therefore unable to meet with George.

B. Many businesspeople in China are not dependable about keeping their appointments.

C. Mr. Li was probably not interested in the products that George was introducing.

D. George failed to identify the one element in Mr. Li's behavior that showed interest.

E. George would have had a greater chance of success had he first developed a greater trust in his relationship with Mr. Li.

Case 2

Understanding the Cultural Background

A woman from China who sells insurance in central Illinois has developed the Asian community as her major clientele (顾客). She has been extremely successful with that group and attributes her success to the cultural and linguistic adaptation of American insurance practices to the values of the Asian clientele. She has business cards and brochures printed in Japanese, Chinese, and Korean; she works very hard at pleasing her clientele. This saleswoman has adapted to the culture of the United States in many ways; she is assertive and outgoing, and she has a good grasp of the concept of profit. She also knows, given her own background, that she must be more indirect and willing to enter into long-term relationships with her clients that in many cases go beyond a typical American business relationship. A number of her clients ask her to give marital advice to their children, act as a go-between in marriage arrangements, and help with other personal matters.

(Adapted from "Intercultural Communication in the Global Workplace" by Iris Varner &

Linda Beamer)

PART ④ Additional Reading

The following is a script of *Chairman Ma*, which was aired on September 28, 2014. Lara Logan is the correspondent.

Jack Ma Brings Alibaba to the U.S.

By now you've probably heard of Alibaba, the Chinese Internet giant which is able to reach millions upon millions of previously unreachable Chinese consumers. The company went public this month on the New York Stock Exchange and became one of the most valuable corporations in the world. And, Alibaba is just getting started.

Everything about the Alibaba's story is unconventional. Let's begin with its founder, Jack Ma, who gained a global celebrity status through the past 10 days as his image became ubiquitous (无处不在的) on business news channels and media outlets across America. We got to know Jack Ma before the onslaught (大量出现的某物), started over a year ago in China, when he talked with us about his relationship with the Chinese government, and his unorthodox (非传统的) business philosophy, which surprisingly gives shareholders almost no say over how he runs the company.

Jack Ma: If you want to invest in us, we believe customer number one, employee number two, shareholder number three. If they don't want to buy that, that's fine. If they regret, they can tell us.

Lara Logan: In the U.S., the shareholder is usually the first.

Jack Ma: Yeah. And I think they were wrong. The shareholders are good. I respect them. But they're the third. Because you've to take care of the customers, take care of the employees, and then shareholders will be taken care of.

Ma's unconventional view didn't stop Wall Street from pouring $25 billion into his company, now listed on the New York Stock Exchange as "BABA." It's an Internet shopping behemoth (巨兽), a collection of online marketplaces where buyers and sellers connect to do business. Most of the company's money comes from advertising and small transaction fees.

On its most popular website, Taobao, users talk to each other, barter (交易) and engage in a way that doesn't happen on American e-commerce websites and Alibaba says there are almost a billion products for sale.

Lara Logan: If I'm buying a house, I can do everything from finding an architect to buying doorknobs to furnishing the entire thing from start to finish. What else?

Jack Ma: Yeah. You can buy anything, as long as it's legal. Anything.

Lara Logan: Five, six years ago, you weren't even making a profit. In fact, in 2002, you made $1 in profit. And today you make how much?

Jack Ma: Billions.

Lara Logan: Billions of dollars.

Jack Ma: Yeah. Yeah.

It's now the biggest e-commerce firm in the world, dwarfing (使…相形见绌) the combined sales of Amazon and eBay. And Alibaba has helped create hundreds of millions of Internet consumers, a whole new social class in China, whose people did not have access to modern commerce before Jack Ma came along.

Lara Logan: And now you have 500 million registered users?

Jack Ma: Yes, yes. It's only, only like a little bit more than 40 percent of China's population and we need more. We have over 100 million people visiting the sites, shopping every day. And it's just the beginning.

When Jack Ma dreamed up Alibaba in 1999, the online world looked nothing like it is today. The most popular search engine was Yahoo, not Google. There were no iPods, iPhones or iPads. Only four out of ten American homes had Internet connections. And the World Wide Web barely reached all the way to China, where retail stores were rare outside the big cities. For most of the country, there was no such thing as package delivery or credit cards. The only way to buy anything was face-to-face and in cash.

Jack Ma: When we started the e-commerce, nobody believed that China would have e-commerce, because people believed in "guan-xi," face-to-face, and all kinds of network in traditional ways. There's not a trust system for e-commerce in China.

He had to overcome centuries of tradition by showing Chinese buyers and sellers that they could trust Alibaba with their money in this new virtual world. He did it by guaranteeing the transactions and creating his own payment system, an escrow account where Alibaba holds the buyers' money until the goods are delivered.

Jack Ma: Every day we finish more than 30 million transactions. And that means that there, you are buying things from somebody you have never seen. You are giving products to the person you have never met. And there are some guys you never know that he's going to take your products to that place, to that person. I want to tell the people that the trust is there.

Lara Logan: Because it's all about trust.

Jack Ma: It's all about the trust.

Now anyone, rich or poor, with access to the Internet and something to sell, can connect with hundreds of millions of potential customers on one of Ma's websites. Ordinary people in China, who never had a way to do business with each other before, today have a stake in the online world. That idea was revolutionary. It created millions of jobs and made Jack Ma a hero to millions of Chinese.

Lara Logan: So this is your old stomping ground (落脚点), right?

Jack Ma: Yeah.

We met Jack Ma in Hangzhou, an ancient city in southeastern China famous for its beauty. This is where he grew up poor in the 1960s, during the Cultural Revolution, when the country was cut off from the West. Then in 1972, Richard Nixon came to Ma's hometown. It was the first visit by a U.S. president to China and the city became a mecca (胜地) for foreign tourists. Through them, 12-year-old Jack got his first glimpse of a world beyond China.

Jack Ma: The name Jack was given by an American tourist.

He told us how he taught himself English, walking up to foreigners and offering free tours in exchange for free lessons. Unlike many successful Chinese entrepreneurs, Jack Ma never studied in the U.S. He also had no status, money or connections. The only other way to get ahead in China was education and he failed the college entrance exam twice.

Jack Ma: My parents do not want me to take examinations again.

Lara Logan: Because they didn't want you to fail again.

Jack Ma: They believed I would fail again.

Lara Logan: How did that affect you?

Jack Ma: That's a good question. Nobody ever asked me how that affected me before. It really affected me a lot. I failed for the first time, and then I asked for looking for jobs. I went to job interviews for about 10 or 15 times and all rejected me.

Lara Logan: Why did everyone reject you?

Jack Ma: I was not the standard, that normal people like...

Lara Logan: Because you were small?

Jack Ma: Normal. I was small.

Lara Logan: And skinny (骨瘦如柴的)?

Jack Ma: Skinny, not handsome and, terrible, the way I talk. And they probably just don't like it.

Ma made it into college on his third try and became an English teacher. With no computing or engineering background, he's an unlikely tech titan but he says he was captivated (迷住) by the Internet from the moment he first saw it in 1995 when he came to the U.S. as a translator.

Jack Ma: I never touched a keyboard before. I never used a computer before. And I say, "What is Internet?" He said, "Jack, you know, search whatever you want on the Internet." I say, "How can I search? What does search mean?" He said, "Just type." I say, "I don't want to type. Computer's so expensive in China, and I don't want to destroy it." He said, "It's not a bomb. Just type." So, I typed the first word called "beer." At that time, very slow, came on the American beer, Japanese beer and the German beer, but not Chinese beers. So, I was curious. And I typed, "China." No China. No data. I came back to Hangzhou with $1 in my pocket, scared and worried. And I came back and I said, "I want to do something called Internet."

His first two ventures failed. Four years later, he convinced some friends and former students, most of whom had never used the Internet, to invest in him and his vision for Alibaba. With just over $50,000 in seed money, the company was born. Today, it is valued at $231 billion and is headquartered in Hangzhou on a sprawling state-of-the-art campus that rivals any in Silicon Valley. Ma's personal fortune makes him the richest man in China and one of the most influential.

But there's another side of him that's little known outside of China, where he's a celebrity. A cult of Ma reaches across the country and inspires almost fanatical loyalty among his employees and their families, who record his speeches and quote his sayings.

Here, he is dressed as a punk rocker performing for an enthusiastic audience of 20,000 Alibaba workers at a company anniversary celebration.

The Chairman Ma show is now playing here in the U.S., bringing with it the potential of hundreds of millions of Chinese consumers for products made in America.

Lara Logan: So this is not Jack Ma's American invasion. This is not for Google, Amazon, eBay... to be afraid.

Jack Ma: We come to help, not invade. For example, bring the U.S.' small bus business to China. This is something that we can do better, because we have 100 million buyers today, every day. We don't know, three years, 300 million?

Questions

1. How much do you know about Jack Ma, the founder of Alibaba?
2. What makes him so successful both at home and abroad?
3. Do you think Alibaba is a good case in point in terms of globalization? Why or why not?

2

Communication and Culture

I do not want my house to be walled in on all sides and my windows to be stuffed. I want cultures of all lands to be blown about my house as freely as possible. But I refuse to be blown off my feet by any.
— *Mahatma Gandhi*

Culture and space separate us, but the need to communicate and the mechanics of communication connect us.

— *L. A. Samovar & R. E. Porter*

Culture is communication and communication is culture.

— *Edward T. Hall*

PART ❶   Warm Up

1. Watch a video clip to get some ideas about the concept of culture.
2. Read the following and try to answer the questions below it.

One afternoon after work, a British teacher of EFL (English as a Foreign Language), who had recently started teaching at a college in Hong Kong, decided to visit some friends who lived in a different part of the city. She went to the appropriate bus stop, and as she walked up, a group of her students who were waiting there asked "Where are you going?" Immediately she felt irritated, and thought to herself, "What business is it of theirs where I'm going? Why should I tell them about my personal life?" However, she tried to hide her irritation, and simply answered, "I'm going to visit some friends."

Several months later this British teacher discovered that "Where are you going?" is simply a greeting in Chinese. There is no expectation that it should be answered clearly: a vague response such as "Over there" or "Into town" is adequate. Moreover, according to Chinese conventions, the students were being friendly and polite in giving such a greeting, not intrusive and disrespectful as the British teacher interpreted them to be.

(Adapted from "Culturally Speaking: Managing Rapport Through Talk Across Cultures"
by Helen Spencer-Oatey)

Questions

1. Why did the British teacher misunderstand her students' friendliness?
2. How many greetings can you think of that Chinese people usually use to greet each other?
3. What are the common greetings that English-speaking people use?

PART ❷ Readings

Passage 1▶ A Wide-Angle View of Communication

From birth to death, all kinds of communication play an integral part in your life. Whatever your occupation or leisure-time activities, communication of one form or another has a role. In fact, if people were asked to analyze how they spend most of their waking day, the most common responses would be "communicating" or "being communicated to." In reality, communication is our link to the rest of humanity.

But what is communication? And what is it we seek to accomplish with communication? Let us begin to answer these questions by examining what we consider to be the essential ingredients of communication.

Senders and receivers. Communication involves people (some scholars call them sources and receivers) who send and receive messages, sometimes simultaneously. This means that the role of sender or receiver is not restricted to any one part in the communication process; instead, we play both roles.

There are times when it seems as if communication is mainly one way: receivers of messages fail to react; senders of messages fail to consider the reactions of the receiver before sending another message. But for communication to be effective, the messages people send to others should, at least in part, be determined by the messages they have received from them.

Field of experience. We each carry our field of experience with us wherever we go. When people with similar life experiences communicate, chances are that they will be able to relate to each other more effectively. However, people whose life experiences differ will probably have difficulty interacting with or understanding one another. As our storehouses of experience diverge ①, it becomes harder for us to share meaning. Conversely, as these storehouses of experience converge ②, the sharing of meaning becomes easier.

Encoding. Encoding is the process of putting an idea into a symbol. The symbols into which you encode your thoughts vary. You can encode thoughts into words, and you can encode thoughts into unspoken symbols. The oils and colors in a painting as well as your gestures and other forms of nonverbal

Notes
① （意见等）分歧
② （趋于）相似或相同

communication can be symbols.

Messages. The message is the content of a communicative act. People communicate a wide variety of messages. Some of these messages are private (a smile accompanied by an "I love you"), while others are directed at millions of people (a network television show, a best seller). Some messages are sent intentionally ("I want you to know"), while others are sent accidentally ("I didn't realize you were watching me"). But as long as someone is there to interpret the results of a sender's efforts, a message is being sent. Thus, we can say that everything a sender does or says has potential message value.

Consequently, whether you smile, listen, renew a book, watch a particular TV program, or turn away from someone, you are communicating some message, and your message is having some effect.

Channels. We may send our messages to receivers through a variety of sensory channels. We may use sound, sight, smell, taste, touch, or any combination thereof to carry a message. Some channels are more effective at communicating messages than others, and the nature of the channel used affects the way a message will be processed. The impact of a message changes as the channel used to transmit it changes. Experience shows that most of us have channel preferences; that is, we prefer to rely on one or more channels while disregarding others. Which channels are you most used to? Why? Adept [3] communicators are channel switchers who recognize that human communication today is an ever-expanding, multi-channeled event.

Noise. Noise is anything that interferes with the ability to send and/or receive messages. Thus, while noise could be sound, it does not necessarily have to be sound. It could also be physical discomfort (a headache), psychological makeup (a poor self-concept, an inflated ego [4], or a high level of defensiveness [5]), semantic [6] misunderstandings (as when people give different meanings to words and phrases or use different words and phrases to mean the same thing), or the environment (a sparsely furnished room, or a dimly lit office).

The important point to remember is that noise can function as a communication barrier. As noise increases, the chances for effective communication usually decrease, and as noise decreases, the chances for effective communication usually rise.

Notes
[3] 内行的
[4] 妄自尊大的自我
[5] 抵触情绪
[6] 语义的

Decoding. Decoding is the opposite process of encoding and just as much an active process. The receiver is actively involved in the communication process by assigning meaning to the symbols received.

Receiver response. It refers to anything the receiver does after having attended to and decoded the message. The response can range from doing nothing to taking some action or actions that may or may not be the action desired by the sender.

Feedback. Feedback returns information to the sender of a message, thereby enabling the sender to determine whether the message was received or correctly understood. There are at least three ways of looking at feedback.

First, it can be positive or negative. Positive feedback encourages sources to continue sending similar messages. In contrast, negative feedback discourages sources from encoding similar messages. Second, feedback can be immediate or delayed; and third, it can be free or limited. In an immediate and free feedback condition, the reactions of the receiver are directly and freely communicated to and perceived by the sender. For example, at a political rally a speaker knows immediately whether the audience in the hall is friendly or unfriendly. In contrast, if you want to communicate your opinion of a newspaper article to the editor, it may be several days or weeks before your views are received by the intended party, and printed.

Feedback is useful for both senders and receivers: it provides senders with the opportunity to measure how they are coming across, and it provides receivers with the opportunity to exert some influence over the communication process.

Effect. Every communication has an outcome; that is, it has some effect on the involved persons, though the effect may not always be immediately observable. The consequence may be monetary, cognitive, physical, or emotional. For example, people may profit from the communication, or learn something, or alter their appearance or self-image.

Context. Finally, every communication takes place in some context, or setting. Sometimes, the context is so natural that we fail to notice it; at other times, the context makes such an impression on us that we make a conscious effort to control our behavior because of it. For example, consider the extent to which your behavior would change if you were to move from a park to a

Notes
⑦ 多维的

political rally, to a movie theater, to a funeral home. Every context provides us with rules or norms for interaction. Sometimes the place, time, and people with us affect us without our ever being aware of it.

So communication is complex and multidimensional ⑦ , and it can be defined in the following way: "Communication is a dynamic, systematic process in which meanings are created and reflected in human interaction with symbols."

(Adapted from "Introducing Intercultural Communication" by Xu Lisheng, and from "Intercultural Communication: An Introduction" by Fred E. Jandt)

Questions

1. What does the author mean by saying that "we play both roles?"
2. What are the essential elements of communication mentioned in the passage?
3. Among these elements, which two do you think are of special significance in intercultural communication? And why?
4. How many Chinese words can you think of that are used to express the concept of "communication?"

Passage 2 ▶ What Culture Means to Us

What does the word *culture* mean to us? It may mean many things. For example, we sometimes say that people who are able to read and write or who know about art, music and literature are cultured. For different people, the word has a different meaning. So we now move from communication to culture. The transition should be a smooth one, for as Hall, an anthropologist ① , reminds us, "Culture is communication and communication is culture."

People learn to think, feel, believe, and act as they do because of the messages that have been communicated to them, and those messages all bear the stamp of culture. This omnipresent ② quality of culture leads Hall to conclude that "there is not one aspect of human life that is not touched and altered by culture." In many ways, Hall is correct: culture is everything and

Notes
① 人类学家
② 普遍存在的

everywhere. And more importantly, at least for our purposes, culture governs and defines the conditions and circumstances under which various messages may or may not be sent, noticed, or interpreted. Remember, we are not born knowing how to dress, what to eat, what toys to play with, which gods to worship, or how to spend our money and our time. Culture is both teacher and textbook. From how much eye contact we employ in conversation to explanations of why we get sick, culture plays a dominant role in our lives. When cultures differ, communication practices may also differ. In modern society different people communicate in different ways, as do people in different societies around the world; and the way people communicate is the way they live. It is their culture. Who talks with whom? How? And about what? These are questions of communication and culture. Communication and culture are inseparable, and culture is the foundation of communication.

Because culture conditions us toward one particular mode of communication over another, it is essential to understand how culture operates as a first step toward improving intercultural communication.

As was the case with communication, many definitions have been suggested for culture. They range from all-encompassing ones ("it is everything") to narrower ones ("it is opera, art, and ballet"), but none seems able to tell us everything about culture. The following definitions are just some of the better-known ones.

- Culture may be defined as what a society does and thinks. —— Sapir, 1921
- What really binds men together is their culture—the ideas and the standards they have in common. —— R. Benedict, 1935
- Culture is man's medium; there is not one aspect of human life that is not touched and altered by culture. This means personality, how people express themselves, including shows of emotion, the way they think, how they move, how problems are solved, how their cities are planned and laid out, how transportation systems function and are organized, as well as how economic and government systems are put together and function.

——Edward T. Hall, 1959

- A culture is a collection of beliefs, habits, living patterns, and behaviors which are held more or less in common by people who occupy particular geographic areas.

—— D. Brown, 1978

Notes
③ 无处不在的
④ 人工制品；手工艺
品

- Culture is the collective programming of the mind which distinguishes the members of one group or society from those of another.

—— G. Hofstede, 1984

- Culture is a mental set of windows through which all of life is viewed. It varies from individual to individual within a society, but it shares important characteristics with members of a society.　　—— L. Beamer & I. Varner, 1995

These and other definitions all point to the fact that culture is all pervasive③, including not only customs and habits, ideas and beliefs but also the artifacts④ made by humans.

(Adapted from "Introducing Intercultural Communication" by Xu Lisheng)

Questions

1. How do you understand "culture is communication and communication is culture?"
2. Among the six definitions given above, which one do you agree with? And why?
3. What have you learned about culture from this passage?

Passage 3 ▶ Images of Culture

There are as many definitions of culture as there are people who have thought about it! We will not try to give another one here, but we will see what is usually mentioned as part of culture. We will also look at some examples that illustrate the different components of culture.

A diagram that helps to define culture is the "onion" (Figure 1), in which a distinction is made between practices and values. Practices or artifacts of culture are the things we choose to have and to do, such as symbols, heroes and rituals.

Figure 1. Onion

Culture: Onion-Diagram

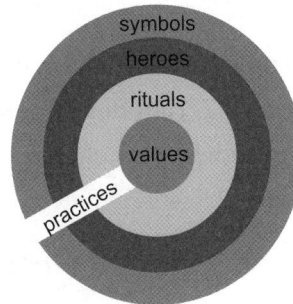

symbols
heroes
rituals
values
practices

(Adopted from Hofstede, 1991)

Symbols: A symbol often used to represent a country is its flag; this flag usually contains another level of symbols that people of that country will recognise (white for the water, and blue for the sky of Finland). Institutions, organizations and companies all have symbols, and knowing why a particular symbol was chosen gives a good idea of the culture of those who chose it. However, the meanings of symbols are not universal: a well-known example is the color black for mourning in some cultures, whereas it is white in other cultures. Some symbols will be easily interpreted in some cultures and not in others. Sometimes they may even have different meanings: "Dame Justitia" with her scale may be recognized as a symbol for justice in many (especially Western) cultures, but a donkey will not always be seen as a symbol of stubbornness by everyone.

Heroes: Heroes are chosen as examples for the people in a particular group, and can be found in their local history, politics, sports or any other field. Very often, the liberator of a country and the founder of an organization are seen as heroes. Some heroes will survive for generations, others, such as music idols, may only last a few years or only a season.

Rituals: Groups of people, as well as individuals, have rituals, the things one is supposed to do in certain situations or at certain moments of the day, the week or the year. A common ritual with many variations is greeting: everywhere in the world, people greet each other, but the ways to do so are very different. Rituals often find their origins in religious traditions.

At the centre of the onion lie the *values*, the reasons why we do what we do, and the reasons behind the practices. These values are the core of the culture, but are more difficult to observe and to know, even in one's own culture.

In order to describe what the values that lie at the core of a culture consist of, Edward T. Hall developed the iceberg analogy of culture in 1976. This iceberg model is now often used as well (Figure 2).

Figure 2. Iceberg

Culture as an Iceberg

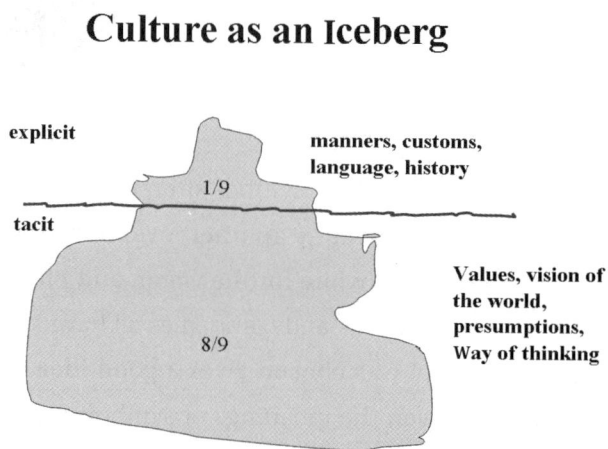

The practices described above are the tip of the iceberg, the things we can see, hear, observe. These practices or artifacts represent one ninth of the iceberg, the small part above the water level that is visible. In it, we can include manners, customs, language: all things we can observe, and hence, learn. We also talk about the explicit aspects of culture, those aspects that we can easily describe.

However, eight ninths of the iceberg, the larger chunk, is hidden under the water level, and we cannot see it. This is where we find the values that underpin [①] the practices, the vision of the world, the ways of thinking, and the assumptions we have. All these aspects are hidden, and they represent tacit knowledge, even in our own culture. This means that we cannot easily express our values: we don't have the concepts, the words to do so, and most of the time we cannot explain why we think something is good or not good, fair or unfair, beautiful or not beautiful. All these things seem 'normal' to us, and what is different is sometimes difficult to accept, all the more so because we

Notes
① 为···打下基础;
支撑

cannot easily express them.

Making mistakes at the tip of the iceberg is relatively safe: very often, people will laugh at a "stupid foreigner who doesn't know how to do it." Mistakes under the water are much more serious and often lead to communication breakdowns, because they clash with what we believe is right, and we don't usually have the words to articulate [2] these value or beliefs.

(Adapted from "Intercultural Communication Introduced" by Marie-Thérèse Claes)

Notes
[2] 阐明；清晰地表达

Questions

1. Why do values lie at the center of the onion?
2. Can you interpret the meanings of the two words *explicit* and *tacit* from the passage?
3. Why are mistakes at the underwater level more serious than those at the tip of the iceberg?

PART ❸   Exercises

Section A   Culture Quiz

1. Watch the video *Collectivism-Individualism Through Dance* to learn some differences between me-culture and we-culture, and explain why the student and the teacher have different opinions on the same answer in the exam.

Me-culture: _____

We-culture: _____

2. **The following is a communication model. Would you please fill in the missing elements based on what you have learned in Passage 1, and then retell the process of communication in your own words?**

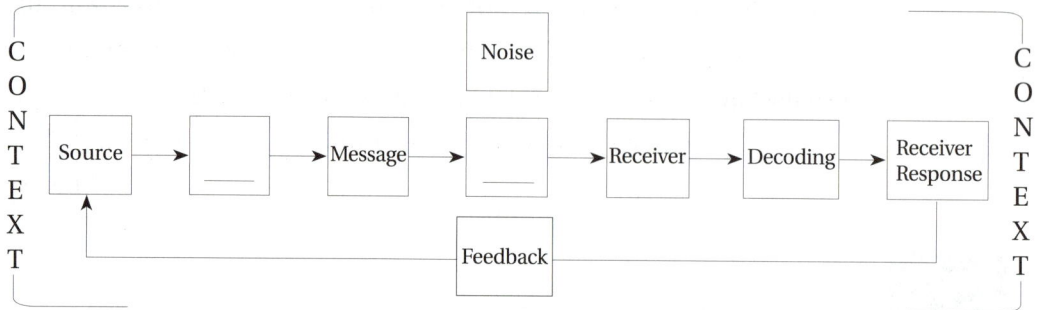

Section **B** Group Discussion

Please form into groups and discuss the following questions with your group members.

1. What's the relationship between communication and culture? Can you provide an example to show this kind of relationship?

2. What are characteristics of communication? And what are characteristics of culture? You can explore them from various sources including the Internet before/after class.

3. What is conveyed in the picture on the right (a Chinese teacher giving a gift to an American teacher)?

Section **C** Intercultural Practice

There are so many definitions of culture we can find in academic books, but most of them are far too abstract to be understood. Some scholars have put forward vivid images to help people understand culture better. Here are some of them. How do you think the following images may help illustrate culture?

1. Culture is like an iceberg.
2. Culture is like the water a fish swims in.
3. Culture is our software.

4. Culture is the story we tell ourselves about ourselves.

5. Culture is the grammar of our behavior.

Section **D** Case Studies

Case 1

Am I a Good Teacher?

Sarah is from Manchester, U.K. She works as a teacher in Xi'an. When she is teaching, she finds students continuously note down what she says in class. In order to let her students relax, she tries to make friends with them, so she invites them to her apartment. She wants to talk with them, but most of the students keep silent.

Then she sees one of the students walk into her study without asking her permission and sit in her favorite chair on which she puts her favorite novel. She feels annoyed, but does not know how to tell the boy. Before she can find a way to tell him, he opens the book and reads it. Sarah cannot bear it, so she says to the boy, "Excuse me. You should ask my permission if you would like to read my book." The boy is very embarrassed and closes the book at once.

Sarah feels depressed, doubts whether she is a good teacher and begins to think about quitting the job since she cannot succeed in teaching these students.

(Adapted from "Intercultural Communication: Case and Analysis" by Hu Sufen & Yang Yali)

Questions

1. What do you think are the causes of the misunderstanding between the British teacher and her boy student?

2. What do you think are the dos and don'ts if you were invited to a foreign teacher's house?

Case 2

First Name or Last Name?

Two men meet on a plane from Tokyo to Hong Kong. Chu Hon-fai is a Hong Kong exporter who is returning from a business trip to Japan. Andrew Richardson is an American buyer on his first business trip to Hong Kong. It is a convenient meeting for them because

Mr. Chu's company sells some of the products Mr. Richardson has come to Hong Kong to buy. After a bit of conversation, they introduce themselves to each other.

Mr. Richardson: By the way, I'm Andrew Richardson. My friends call me Andy. This is my business card.

Mr. Chu: I'm David Chu. Pleased to meet you, Mr. Richardson. This is my card.

Mr. Richardson: No, no. Call me Andy. I think we'll be doing a lot of business together.

Mr. Chu: Yes, I hope so.

Mr. Richardson (reading Mr. Chu's card): "Chu, Hon-fai." Hon-fai, I'll give you a call tomorrow as soon as I get settled at my hotel.

Mr. Chu (smiling): Yes. I'll expect your call.

When these two men separate, they leave each other with divergent impressions of the situation. Mr. Richardson is very pleased to have made the acquaintance of Mr. Chu and feels they have gotten off to a very good start. They have established their relationship on a first-name basis and Mr. Chu's smile seems to indicate that he will be friendly and easy to do business with. Mr. Richardson is particularly pleased that he has treated Mr. Chu with respect for his Chinese background by calling him Hon-fai rather than using his Western name, David, which seemed to him an unnecessary imposition of Western culture.

In contrast, Mr. Chu feels quite uncomfortable with Mr. Richardson. He feels it will be difficult to work with him, and that Mr. Richardson might be rather insensitive to cultural differences. He is particularly bothered that Mr. Richardson used his given name, Hon-fai, instead of either David or Mr. Chu. It was this embarrassment which caused him to smile.

(Adapted from "Intercultural Communication: A Discourse Approach" by Scollon &
Scollon)

Questions

1. Why did they have different impressions when Mr. Chu and Mr. Richardson parted?
2. Do you think culture played a role in the communication between these two men? Why or why not?

Case 3

Friends Were Friends Forever?

Steve and Yaser first met in their chemistry class at an American university. Yaser was an international student from Jordan. He was excited to know an American, and because he wanted to learn more about American culture, Yaser hoped that he and Steve would become good friends.

At first, Steve seemed very friendly. He always greeted Yaser warmly before class. Sometimes he offered to study with Yaser. He even invited Yaser to have lunch with him. But after the semester was over, Steve seemed more distant. The two former classmates didn't see each other very much at school. One day Yaser decided to call Steve. Steve didn't seem very interested in talking to him. Yaser was hurt by Steve's change of attitude. "Steve said we were friends," Yaser complained. "And I said friends were friends forever."

(Adapted from "Intercultural Communication in English" by Xu Lisheng)

Questions

1. What was wrong in the relationship between Yaser and Steve? In your opinion, who, Yaser or Steve, is to be blamed for it? And why?
2. How much do you know about the way Americans view friendship?
3. What tips would you like to offer to non-Americans who want to be friends with Americans?

PART ❹ Additional Reading

What does culture do for human beings? Why do we need culture? What functions does culture serve? Read the following passage and try to get some idea about the five functions of culture: identity meaning, group inclusion, intergroup boundary regulation, ecological adaptation, and cultural communication.

Functions of Culture

As an essential component of the effort of human beings to survive and thrive in their particular environment, culture serves multiple functions.

First, culture serves the **identity meaning function**. Culture provides the frame of reference to answer the most fundamental question of every human being: Who am I? Cultural beliefs, values, and norms provide the anchoring points in which we attribute meanings and significance to our identities. For example, in the larger U.S. culture, middle-class U.S. values emphasize individual initiative (首创精神) and achievement. A person is considered "competent" or "successful" when he or she takes the personal initiative to realize his or her full potential. The translation of this potential means tangible (有形的) achievements and rewards (e.g., an enviable career, a good salary, a coveted car, or a dream house). A person who can realize his or her dreams despite difficult circumstances is considered to be a "successful" individual in the context of middle-class U.S. culture.

The concept of being a "successful" "competent" or "worthwhile" person and the meanings attached to such words stem from the fundamental values of a given culture. The identity meanings we acquire within our culture are constructed and sustained through everyday communication. For example, in the Chinese culture, the meaning of being a "worthwhile" person means that the individual respects his or her parents at all times and is sensitive to the needs of his or her family. In the Mexican culture, a "well-educated" person means that the person has been well taught by his or her parents the importance of demonstrating social relationships with respect and dignity.

Second, culture serves the **group inclusion function**, satisfying our need for membership affiliation (从属关系) and belonging. Culture creates a comfort zone in which we experience in-group inclusion and in-group/out-group differences. Within our own group, we experience safety, inclusion, and acceptance. We do not have to constantly justify or explain our actions. With people of dissimilar groups, we have to be on the alert and we have to explain or defend our actions with greater effort.

However, with people from a dissimilar membership group, we constantly have to perform guessing games. We tend to "stand out," and we experience awkwardness during interaction. The feeling of exclusion or differentiation leads to interaction anxiety and uncertainty. The urge toward group inclusion addresses our need to be seen as similar to others and fit in with them. The group inclusion need also creates boundaries between "us" and "them."

Third, culture's **intergroup boundary regulation function** shapes our in-group and out-group attitudes in dealing with people who are culturally dissimilar. An "attitude" is a learned tendency that influences our behavior. Culture helps us to form evaluative attitudes toward in-group and out-group interactions. We tend to hold favorable attitudes toward in-group interactions and hold unfavorable attitudes toward out-group interactions. We tend to experience strong emotional reactions when our cultural norms are violated or ignored. We tend to experience bewilderment when we unintentionally violate other people's cultural norms. While our own culture builds an invisible boundary around us, it also delimits (定⋯界) our thoughts and our visions.

Culture is like a pair of sunglasses. It shields us from external harshness and offers us some measure of safety and comfort. It also blocks us from seeing clearly through our tinted lenses (有色镜片) because of that same protectiveness. In brief, culture nurtures our ethnocentric(民族文化中心主义的) attitudes and behaviors. The term "ethnocentrism" refers to our tendency to consider our own cultural practices as superior and consider other cultural practices as inferior. As cultural beings, we are all ethnocentric to some degree. We often consider our own cultural way of seeing and sensing as much more "civilized" and "correct" than other cultural ways.

Fourth, culture serves the **ecological adaptation function**. It facilitates (促进) the adaptation processes among the self, the cultural community, and the larger environment. Culture is not a static system. It is dynamic and changes with the people within the system. Culture evolves with a clear reward and punishment system that reinforces certain adaptive behaviors and punishes other non-adaptive behaviors over time. When people adapt their needs and their particular ways of living in response to a changing habitat, culture also changes accordingly. Surface-level cultural artifacts such as fashion or popular culture change at a faster pace than deep-level cultural elements such as beliefs, values, and ethics. Culture rewards certain behaviors that are compatible with its ecology and punishes other behaviors that are mismatched with its ecological niche (生态龛、生态位).

Fifth and finally, culture serves the **cultural communication function**, which basically means the coordination between culture and communication. Culture affects communication, and communication affects culture, just as Hall points out "Culture is communication and communication is culture." It is through communication that culture is passed down, created, and modified from one generation to the next. Communication is necessary to define cultural experiences. Cultural communication shapes the implicit theories we have about appropriate human conduct and effective human practices in a given sociocultural context.

Cultural communication provides us with a set of ideals of how social interaction can be accomplished smoothly among people within our community. For example, people in a particular speech community have established a set of norms of what constitutes a polite or impolite way of meeting strangers. In Western Apache (阿帕切族，美国西南部一印第安部族名) culture, remaining silent is the most proper way to behave when strangers meet.

In sum, culture serves as the "safety net" in which individuals seek to satisfy their needs for identity, inclusion, boundary regulation, adaptation, and communication coordination. Culture facilitates and enhances individuals' adaptation processes in their natural cultural habitats. Communication, in essence, serves as the primary means of linking these diverse needs together.

(Adapted from "Communicating Across Cultures" by Stella Ting-Toomey)

Questions

1. Could you put these five functions of culture into Chinese?
2. Aside from the functions mentioned in the passage, do you know any other function of culture?

Verbal Communication

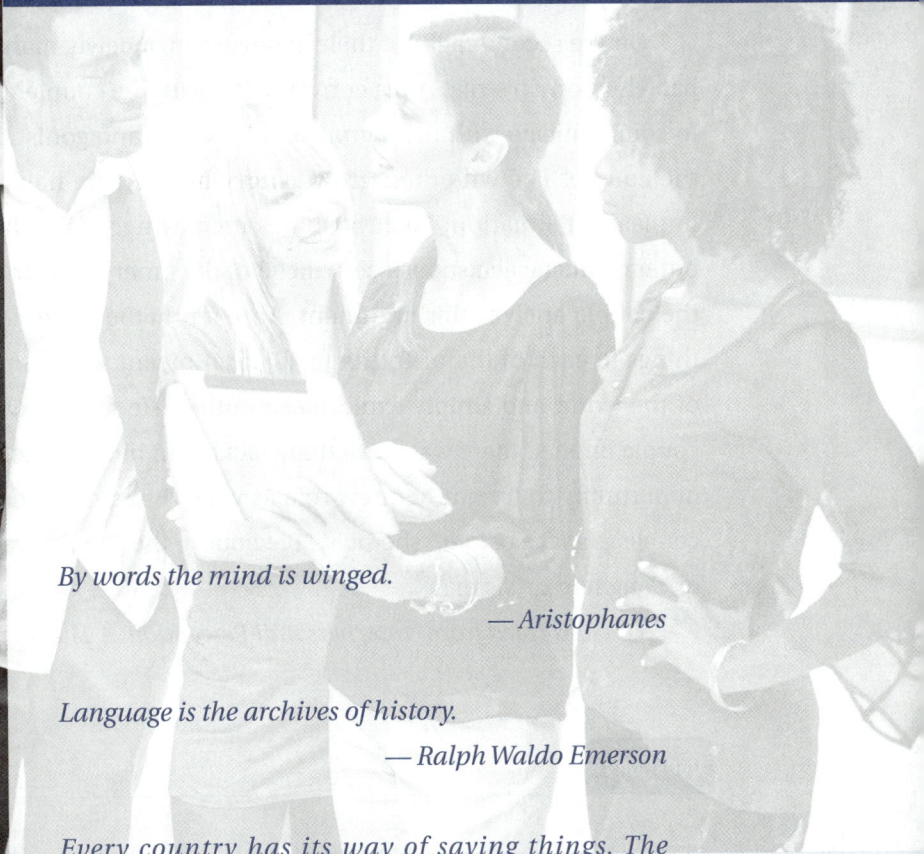

By words the mind is winged.

— Aristophanes

Language is the archives of history.

— Ralph Waldo Emerson

Every country has its way of saying things. The important thing is that which lies behind people's words.

— Freya Stark

PART ❶ Warm Up

1. Watch a video clip to get some ideas about the verbal communication.
2. Read the following story and answer the questions below it.

On the second night of their honeymoon, a newly married couple are sitting at a hotel bar. The woman strikes up a conversation with the couple next to her. The husband refuses to communicate with the couple and becomes antagonistic (敌对的) toward his wife and the couple. The wife then grows angry because he has created such an awkward and unpleasant situation. Each becomes increasingly disturbed, and the evening ends in a bitter conflict, each spouse convinced of the other's lack of consideration. Eight years later, the couple analyze this argument. Apparently the word *honeymoon* had meant different things to each of them. To the husband it meant a golden opportunity to ignore the rest of the world and simply explore each other. He felt his wife's interaction with the other couple implied there was something lacking in him. To the wife her honeymoon meant an opportunity to try out her new role as wife. "I had never had a conversation with another couple as a wife before," she says. "Previous to this I had always been a 'girlfriend' or 'fiancée' or 'daughter' or 'sister'."

(Adapted from "Interpersonal Perception: A Theory and a Method of Research" by H. Phillipson & A. R. Lee)

Questions

1. What's wrong with the newly married couple?
2. How did the confusion arise?
3. How much do you know about verbal communication?

PART ❷ Readings

Passage ❶ ▶ Verbal Language in Intercultural Communication

The importance of language to the study of intercultural communication is clearly captured in Henry Ward Beecher's sentence "Thought is the blossom; language the opening bud; action the fruit behind it." Our ability to make sounds and marks allows us to exchange ideas, to express views, to see information, and to express feelings. Through our use of sounds and symbols, we give life to our ideas. The richness and expressive versatility of language was observed by Paul Tillich when he once wrote "Language has created the word 'loneliness' to express the pain of being alone and the word 'solitude' to express the joy of being alone." So our task in this unit is to develop an understanding and appreciation of verbal language as it functions in intercultural communication.

Language is important to human interaction so much so that we take speaking and writing for granted; that is, we frequently overlook the significant influence language has on human behavior. Over millions of years, we have evolved the organ necessary to produce and receive sounds; in a much shorter span of time, we have created cultural systems in which those sounds have taken on meaning by representing things, feelings, and ideas. Culture and language are intertwined, and they certainly make an attractive couple, as in the chicken and egg dilemma — which came first, the language or the culture? Culture is communication, and culture has such a pervasive influence on communication. In intercultural context, communication gets complicated like everything else. What people say, how they say it, what they don't say — and especially what they mean by what they say — are all deeply affected by culture.

Languages are not neutral codes and grammatical rules. When selecting words, forming sentences, and sending a message, either oral or written, one also makes cultural choices. Thus cultural diversity in language behavior remains one of the most difficult and persistent problems encountered in intercultural communication. Undoubtedly teaching culture has to cover a wide range of studies on how language is used and how its form and function change across different cultures. For this reason, we examine two prominent issues of verbal language in intercultural communication: 1) principles of verbal messages; 2) intercultural effects upon language use.

Language may serve different functions in different situations, but all utterances are multi-functional. A speaker might focus on the meaning of language used by saying, for example: "Go and look it up in the dictionary!" But it is also a directive; it tells someone to do something. Language with a constant function focuses on the channels of communication, as when a speaker says: "Can you hear me?" These verbal messages are particularly relevant to the speaker's communicative concern. People are constantly monitoring each other's behavior, interpreting it, reading between the lines, and so on. However, in intercultural communication verbal language may not serve the expected function because of different communicative styles — by being either direct or indirect, or because of cultural differences. Confusion can result when we look for the meaning in the words and not in the person, and misunderstanding may occur in situations due to cultural differences. This confusion and misunderstanding is one of the outcomes when verbal messages fail to communicate their intended meanings.

Additionally, in the process of intercultural communication, verbal language may borrow extensively from other languages, and may also experience changes in both form and function. To communicate with one another, people are forced to find a *lingua franca* (contact language). English today serves as a lingua franca in many parts of the world. But social factors have greatly influenced the language. Varieties such as Singaporean English, Australian English, and Chinese English have emerged as the products of multicultural exchanges. Attitudes toward Chinese English will likely change as China acquires greater global influence.

(Adapted from "An Introduction to Sociolinguistics" by Ronald Wardhaugh, and from "Communication Between Cultures" by L. A. Samovar, R. E. Porter & L. A. Stefani)

Questions

1. What is the importance of verbal languages in communication?
2. What is the relationship between a culture and its verbal language?

3. Why may verbal language sometimes fail to communicate its intended meaning?

4. What are the characteristics of Chinese English? Try to name at least two of them.

5. What are the problems with the two posts below? What are the causes of those mistakes?

Passage 2 ▶ Direct and Indirect Communication Styles

Notes

① 低语境文化语境是使用语言的环境，包括一切主客观因素。美国人类学家 Edward T. Hall 在 1976 年出版的《超越文化》一书中，提出文化具有语境性，并将语境分为高语境和低语境（所谓低语境是指，一切都需要用语言讲清楚，也就是说双方并没有分享一个共同的语境）

② 个人主义的（一种道德的、政治的和社会的哲学，认为个人利益应是决定行为的最主要因素，强调个人的自由和个人权利的重要性）

Most cultures have a number of forms of polite usage, which can be misleading. For instance, Americans often ask questions to give orders or requests (Would you like to …?). In all cultures there are certain words or types of conversation, which are considered appropriate for certain situations, e.g. introducing people to one another or asking someone for a favour. There are differences in the amount of directness or indirectness one chooses as well as differences in the structure of conversations. The usual question-answer speech sequence is not used in all cultures, and negations (the word "no") are not used in some Asian countries. In any case, language fluency is a necessary condition for functional intercultural communication.

It is not useful to describe any culture as having a direct or indirect communication style because most cultures exhibit both. However, the degree to which one is preferred differs from culture to culture. In a direct communication style, speakers say what they mean and mean what they say; there is no need to read between the lines; it's best to tell it like it is; speakers are less likely to imply and more likely to say exactly what they think; yes means yes. Direct styles are often used in low-context ①, individualistic ② cultures. Cultures such as the United States, England, Australia, and Germany, prefer the direct style. In the United States, people often use the expression "for sure," "no question," "without doubt." Verbal precision and self-expression are valued. In intercultural business negotiation settings, American negotiators are mission-driven, and they express their offers openly. They may say "Let's go to the point," or "Speak up, what do you think?" They like to be openly challenged for the negotiation, and they think it is quite normal if they run into conflict with any party concerned. Their style of negotiation comes from their direct communication preference.

However, in an indirect communication style, speakers don't always say what they mean or mean exactly what they say; listeners have to read between the lines; speakers are more likely to suggest or imply than to come out and say what they think; listeners can't always tell it like it is (what if that upsets the other person?); yes may mean maybe or even no. Indirect communication style is often seen in high-context ③ and collectivistic ④ cultures, and using ambiguous and vague words is the characteristic of this style. In high-context cultures, there is no need to tell every message. True understanding is implicit, coming not from words but from actions in the environment. Moreover, indirect communication may prevent embarrassment to either speaker. Many Asian countries, such as China and Japan, use an indirect style. Saving face and maintaining harmony in social relationships are highly valued in these cultures, so direct expressions of one's need are avoided to lessen the possibility of conflict. Compared with American negotiators who follow the direct style, Chinese negotiators usually look forward to long-term partnership. Generally there is a slow "warm up," followed by tentative suggestions. Chinese negotiators don't enter negotiations anticipating conflict, and they are always trying to "save face" for both parties.

While both direct and indirect features are present in any culture, direct modes of communication are preferred in cultures like the United States, whereas indirect modes are used most often in many Asian cultures, such as Japan, Korea, and China. The following dialogue takes place between a young couple who have been dating for a short time. The man is a student from the U.S., and the woman is from an Asian country. Note the misunderstanding that results from the use of direct and indirect modes of communication.

Jim: You know, Michiko. I really enjoy the time we spend together. I really like you. I've been so happy since we met.

Notes

③ 高语境文化（所谓高语境是指，许多意思都包括在语境之中，不需要将每一点都明白无误地讲出来）

④ 集体主义的（主张个人从属于社会的一种思想理论，其科学含义在于，当个人利益和集体利益发生矛盾时，前者要服从后者）

Michiko:	Hmmm, thank you.
Jim:	I mean, I feel like I've learned so much about you and your culture.
Michiko:	Yeah, it's very interesting.
Jim:	I'm so glad you came to the United States. Do you like it here?
Michiko:	Well, it's pretty big. It's very nice here.
Jim:	What do you think about Americans?
Michiko:	I don't know. Maybe I haven't been here long enough to know.
Jim:	You must think of something.
Michiko:	Well, I'd probably have to think about it.
Jim:	I mean, do you like us?
Michiko:	Well, I don't really know that many Americans yet.

In all likelihood, Jim is not going to get much of an answer from Michiko. She continues, throughout the dialogue, using rather general answers to Jim's very specific and direct questions about her feelings toward the United States. Michiko might believe that Jim is being far too direct and invading her privacy. Besides, she hasn't been in the United States long enough. Michiko cannot possibly say something critical about the United States because she would lose face as a non-native. She relies on imprecise and indefinite answers, which frustrates Jim.

Summing it all up, verbal intercultural communication happens when people from different cultural backgrounds communicate with each other through language. It is argued that language helps in communicating with people from different backgrounds. However, people may be less aware that cultural literacy is necessary in order to understand the language being used. In case of using a term or phrase without being aware of its cultural implications, one may at best communicate poorly and at worst send entirely wrong messages. Therefore, words in themselves do not carry the meaning. The meaning comes out of the context, the cultural usage. Although people use a dictionary to explain one language's words in another language, literal translation often doesn't mean the same thing because of each culture's influence on the word's meaning. Cultures influence not only vocabulary, but also the way it is used. Knowing the different ways of addressing, greeting and giving compliments greatly improves the intercultural communication.

(Adapted from "Figuring Foreigners Out: A Practical Guide" by Craig Storti)

Passage ▶3 Addressing People

How to address people is always the first problem to be solved in intercultural communication. English and Chinese have different rules for the order of family names and given names. For Chinese, surnames come first and given names second. But for Westerners, it is just the opposite. Chinese people would like to address others by their full names, but English people often address others by their given names if they know each other. In 1989, Deng Yanchang stated that in recent years, the trend of many English-speaking people has been to address others by using the first name — Tom, Michael, Linda, Jane, etc. — rather than calling the person Mr. Summers, Mrs. Howard or Miss Jones. This is especially common among Americans, even when people meet for the first time. This applies not only to people of roughly the same age, but also of different ages. This may even include the children's parents or grand-parents. It is clear that this is not a sign of disrespect. People of different social status are doing the same. For example, many college students call their professors by their first name. The professors do not regard this as a sign of disrespect or familiarity, but rather, as a sign of an indication that the professor is considered affable and has a sense of equality. This, of course, is contrary to Chinese customs. One can imagine the reaction of adults if a child were to call a grandparent by his or her name, or a student to do the same in calling a teacher.

Chinese people always value factors such as being polite and being respectful in addressing people. Born and brought up in a society of rigid hierarchy, Chinese are always careful in choosing appropriate titles. Assuming Westerners have the same pattern in addressing, many Chinese students address their foreign English teachers in a very Chinese way. For example, when an American says "Good morning, everyone!" to a class, most probably, he or she will receive a reply as "Good morning, teacher." From the primary school to high school, Chinese students are used to saying "*Laoshi hao*! (老师好！)" which means "Hello, teacher!" This is a sign of showing respect to teachers. In such a case, what the American teacher feels is discomfort rather than being respected.

Moreover, Chinese have other problems in addressing foreigners. Very often, they confuse foreigners' family names and do not know that it is a rule that surname alone is not normally an acceptable form of address. Though it is true that some foreigners in China prefer to call the Chinese people directly by their surnames for the sake of convenience, it would be wrong if Chinese draw a conclusion that it is acceptable to call a person by his surname in English. Take Linda Jane Chapman for example, if you address this lady Chapman or Miss Linda, she will feel uncomfortable.

Some Chinese think that to call a foreigner by his given name implies intimacy and friendliness. In fact, it is not the case. The relationship does not have to be very intimate. Research shows that there is an increasing tendency among Western young people to use their given names in all situations except the most formal ones.

As a result of these differences, Chinese people feel uncomfortable to use a Westerner's given name, especially when they want to keep a social distance from the Westerner or when they want to be respectful to him or her. On the other hand, Westerners feel alienated to be consistently called by the family name, which is a symbol to maintain a gap between them. Understanding the differences in addressing people, Chinese and Westerners would have fewer problems in communicating with each other.

(Adapted from "Log Into the World of Cultures — Intercultural Communication" by Zhang Ailin and from "A Study on Intercultural Communication" by Zhao Yunlong)

Questions

1. What kind of different rules do the English and Chinese have for the order of family names and given names?

2. Is it acceptable for Western children to address their parents or grand-parents by using their given names? Why or why not?

3. Is it acceptable for Chinese college students to address their professors by using their given names? Why or why not?

PART ❸ Exercises

Section A ▶ Culture Quiz

Below are 32 statements regarding how a person may feel about communicating. Please indicate the degree to which you agree or disagree with each statement. If you strongly disagree with the statement, please mark "1" in the blank before the statement; if you strongly agree, mark "9;" if you are unsure or find that the item does not apply to you, mark "5" in the blank.

(Strongly Disagree)←1 2 3 4 5 6 7 8 9→(Strongly Agree)

1. _____ I catch on to what others mean, even when they do not say it directly.

2. _____ I show respect to superiors, even if I dislike them.

3. _____ I use my feelings to determine whether to trust another person.

4. _____ I find silence awkward in a conversation.

5. _____ I communicate in an indirect fashion.

6. _____ I use many colorful words when I talk.

7. _____ In argument, I insist on very precise definitions.

8. _____ I avoid clear-cut expressions of feelings when I communicate with others.

9. _____ I am good at figuring out what others think of me.

10. _____ My verbal and nonverbal speech tends to be very dramatic.

11. _____ I listen attentively, even when others are talking in an uninteresting manner.

12. _____ I maintain harmony in my communication with others.

13. _____ Feelings are a valuable source of information.

14. _____ When pressed for an opinion, I respond with an ambiguous statement/position.

15. _____ I try to adjust myself to the feelings of the person with whom I am communicating.

16. _____ I actively use a lot of facial expressions when I talk.

17. _____ My feelings tell me how to act in a given situation.

18. _____ I am able to distinguish between a sincere invitation and one intended as a gesture of politeness.

19. _____ I believe that exaggerated stories make a conversation fun.

20. _____ I orient to people through my emotions.

21. _____ I find myself initiating conversations with strangers while waiting in line.

22. _____ As a rule, I openly express my feelings and emotions.

23. _____ I feel uncomfortable and awkward in social situations in which everybody else is talking except me.

24. _____ I readily reveal personal things about myself.

25. _____ I like to be accurate when I communicate.

26. _____ I can read another person "like a book."

27. _____ I use silence to avoid upsetting others when I communicate.

28. _____ I openly show my disagreement with others.

29. _____ I am a very precise communicator.

30. _____ I can sit with another person, not say anything, and still be comfortable.

31. _____ I think that un-talkative people are boring.

32. _____ I am an extremely open communicator.

Scoring: Reverse the score for items 4, 6, 7, 10, 16, 19, 21, 22, 23, 24, 25, 28, 29, 31, 32. If your original score was 1, reverse it to a 7; if your original score was a 2, reverse it to a 6; etc. After reversing the score for those 14 items, simply sum the 32 items. Lower scores indicate low context communication (direct style). Higher scores indicate high context communication (indirect style).

(Adapted from "The Influence of Cultural Individualism-Collectivism, Self Construals, and Individual Values on Communication Styles Across Cultures" by W. B. Gudykunst, Y. Matsumoto, S. Ting-Toomey, et al.)

Section **B** Group Discussion

Directness and indirectness in communication styles probably account more for intercultural misunderstanding than any other single factor. Now identify cultural differences in the following dialogues.

Saturday Shift

Ms. Jones: It looks like we're going to need some people to come in on Saturday.

Mr. Wu: I see.

Ms. Jones: Can you come in on Saturday?

Mr. Wu: Yes, I think so.

Ms. Jones: That'll be a great help.

Mr. Wu: Yes. Saturday's a special day, did you know?

Ms. Jones: How do you mean?

Mr. Wu: It's my son's birthday.

Ms. Jones: How nice. I hope you all enjoy it very much.

Mr. Wu: Thank you. I appreciate your understanding.

A Bit of a Nuisance

Gitti: How did it go with Arabella?

Karl: Much better than I expected.

Gitti: Did you explain everything to her?

Karl: Yes. I said that we were very sorry but we weren't going to be able to meet the deadline.

Gitti: What did she say?

Karl: She just said "That's a bit of a nuisance" and started talking about something else.

Gitti: That's a relief.

(Adapted from "Figuring Foreigners Out: A Practical Guide" by Craig Stortie)

Section C ► Intercultural Practice

You are going to compare direct and indirect styles of communication. In the following exercise, you are presented with a series of statements made by direct communicators. Imagine the setting to be a meeting in a certain culture (where maintaining harmony and saving face are very important), and switch the direct style into the indirect style. The first one has been done for you.

1. I'm not sure that's such a good idea.
   - Do you think that's a good idea?
   - Are there any other ideas?
   - I like most parts of that idea.
2. That's not exactly the point.
3. I think we should…
4. Those figures are not completely accurate.
5. That's not the way to do that.
6. I don't agree.

(Adapted from "Figuring Foreigners Out: A Practical Guide" by Craig Stortie)

Section D ► Case Studies

Case 1

An Initial Problem

It seems a little old lady was seeking a house in Switzerland. She asked the local village schoolmaster to help her. A place that suited her was finally found, and the little lady returned to London for her baggage. She remembered then that she hadn't noticed a bathroom, or as she called it, a "water closet." So, she wrote to the village schoolmaster and asked if there was a "W. C." in or near the house.

The schoolmaster was puzzled by the initials — never dreamed, of course, that she was asking about a bathroom. He finally asked the help of the parish priest. The priest decided that she was asking about a wayside chapel (路边的小拜堂).

Imagine the shock caused in the mind of the little old lady when she read the following letter from the schoolmaster.

Dear Madam,

The W. C. is situated just nine miles from the house in the center of a beautiful grove of trees. It is capable of holding 350 people at one time, and is open Tuesdays, Thursdays, and Sundays each week. A large number of people attend during the summer months, so it is suggested that you go early, although there is plenty of standing room.

Some folks like to take their lunch and make a day of it, especially on Thursdays when there is organ (风琴) accompaniment (伴奏). The acoustics (音响效果) are very excellent, and everyone can hear the slightest sound.

It may interest you to know that my daughter met her husband the first time in the W. C., and later they were married in this same W. C.

We hope that you will be here in time for one of our bazaars (义卖) to be held very soon — the proceeds (所得收入) will go toward the purpose of buying plush (豪华的) seats, which the folks have long felt are needed, as the present seats all have holes in them.

My wife is a very delicate person, and therefore, she cannot attend regularly. It has been six months since she last went. Naturally, it pains her very much not going more often.

I will now close with a desire to accommodate you in any way possible, and I will be happy to save you a seat in the front or near the door, whichever you wish.

Yours sincerely,

School Master

Questions

1. What has caused the misunderstanding between the school master and the old lady?
2. Which word is most widely used in America to mean a toilet in a public building?
3. Which word is most widely used in America to mean a toilet in the private house?

Case 2

A Misunderstanding at the Dinner Table

Roger was a student majoring in East Asia Studies in an American university. He started an e-mail correspondence with Li Zhang, a sociology major in China, who was introduced to him through a mutual friend.

Upon graduation, Roger received a generous gift from his grandfather—Grandpa would pay for a round-trip ticket to China. He told Li Zhang the good news, and the two decided to meet.

Li Zhang decided to give Roger a very special welcome: she and the three students from her dormitory would cook him an authentic Chinese meal, as Roger had told her that he loved Chinese food.

However, when Roger was presented with the dinner, he was almost terrified by some of the food: pork stomach soup, pig liver with ginger and spring onion, and chicken with mushrooms in which the chicken had been cut to pieces with bones still attached.

Fortunately, there were courses like tofu (bean curd), stir-fried beef, steamed fish and vegetables that Roger loved. He tried to stick to them, but Li Zhang kept putting food he did not like on his plate. When she asked how he liked the liver, Roger said, "It's very unusual ... and interesting." This seemed to make Li Zhang happy, and she gave him more liver. Roger tried to stop her, but she would not be stopped. Roger was so frustrated that he told her that he did not really like it that much.

"But you said it was unusual and interesting!" Li Zhang said.

"Well, they both mean something less than positive," Roger said carefully, trying not to hurt their feelings.

Li Zhang and her friends became concerned at this. "So you don't like the food?"

"I'm not used to eating liver, that's all. But I do like the chicken, the beef, the tofu, and the vegetables. I have had more than enough to eat. I never make this much food at home," Roger was eager to let them know how much he appreciated their effort. "Trust me, I'm enjoying the food. I know what I like."

Having said that, he found a piece of chicken that was less bony, held it in his hands to eat it, and then licked his fingers.

Li Zhang and her friends looked at each other in shock.

It was not an ideal first meeting for either Li Zhang or Roger.

(Adapted from "Cultures in Contrast: Miscommunication and Misunderstanding Between Chinese and North Americans" by Dai Fan & Stephen L. J. Smith)

Questions

1. Why did Li Zhang keep putting food onto Roger's plate?
2. What cultural differences can you identify in this case?

Case 3

Was She Always Lying?

Ms Zhang was a baby-sitter in a German family living in China. She got on well with the whole family at the beginning though her English was very limited. Ms. Zhang was a good cook and the whole family was very pleased with her delicious food. However, before the dinner, she always said to them: "I am sorry that I am a poor cook. Please try the dishes cooked by me. If they are bad, please forgive my fault." The German couple was surprised to hear what she said for the first time, because the dishes were unexpectedly very delicious. However, she repeated it as a rule whenever she put the dishes on the table. The couple's confusion finally led to the belief that Ms. Zhang was hollow-hearted. They could not understand why she was lying.

Questions

1. Could you explain to the German couple why Ms. Zhang said she was a poor cook when she was actually a good one?
2. What advice would you give to the both sides to overcome the misunderstanding?

PART ❹   Additional Reading

Cultural Differences in Verbal Communication

When we want to assert ourselves as unique (individualism), we must be direct so that others will know where we stand. To describe themselves to others, individualists must be direct. Indirect communication, however, often is used in intimate relationships (e.g., to express emotions). If our goal is to maintain harmony in the group (collectivism), we cannot be direct because we might offend another member of the group. To maintain harmony, collectivists need to be cautious and indirect. Indirect communication, therefore, predominates in collectivistic cultures whenever maintaining harmony is important. When maintaining harmony is not a primary concern, collectivists often use direct communication.

Cultural Differences in Direct Language Usage. Analytic thinking (分析性思维) tends to predominate in the United States, and synthetic thinking (综合性思维) tends to predominate in China. *Analytic thinking* involves looking at parts, rather than focusing on the whole. *Synthetic thinking*, in contrast, involves trying to grasp things in their totality. Constructing low-context messages requires analytic thinking, and constructing high-context messages involves synthetic thinking. Analytic thinking leads to the use of linear reasoning in talking or writing because it is necessary to specify how the parts are related to each other. Synthetic thinking leads to a more ambiguous or implicit logic. According to Okabe, "The speaker organizes his or her ideas in a stepping-stone mode: The listener is supposed to supply what is left unsaid."

Cultural differences in direct and indirect forms of communication can be illustrated further by comparing the United States and Japan:

Reflecting the cultural value of precision, Americans' tendency to use words explicitly is the most noteworthy in their communicative style. They prefer to employ such categorical words as "absolutely," "certainly," and "positively." The English syntax dictates that the absolute "I" be placed at the beginning of the sentence in most cases, and that the subject-predicate relation be constructed in an ordinary sentence. … By contrast, the cultural assumptions of interdependence and harmony require that Japanese speakers limit themselves to implicit and even ambiguous use of words. In order to avoid leaving an assertive impression, they like to depend more frequently on qualifiers such as "maybe" "perhaps" "probably" and "somewhat." Since Japanese syntax does not require the use of a subject in a sentence, the qualifier predicate is the predominant form of sentence construction.

These differences are often manifested even when Japanese speak in English and Americans speak in Japanese.

It is important to recognize that indirectness occurs in individualistic cultures like the United States too. The reasons for indirectness in individualistic cultures like the United States, however, appear to be different than those in collectivistic cultures. A professional interpreter in Japan says:

Americans can be just as indirect as the Japanese, but they are indirect about different things, and being indirect carries a different meaning. Americans are usually indirect when something very sensitive is being discussed or when they are nervous about how the other person might react. Whenever Americans are indirect, I suspect that something is going on!

Japanese indirectness is a part of our way of life. It is not because we are such kind and considerate people that we worry about other's reactions. It is just that we know our own fates and fortunes are always bound up with others. I think you can value directness when you value individualism, or when you are with people you know and trust completely.

Americans are indirect at times and Japanese also are direct, most frequently in close friendships.

(Adapted from "Bridging Differences — Effective Intergroup Communication" by William B. Gudykunst)

Questions

1. What are the differences between analytic thinking and synthetic thinking?
2. Can you illustrate the cultural differences in direct and indirect forms of communication by comparing the United States with China?
3. What do you think silence means in Chinese culture? Is it the same in Japanese culture?

Nonverbal Communication

There's language in her eye, her cheek, her lip; Nay, her foot speaks; her wanton spirits look out at every joint and motive of her body.

— William Shakespeare

What you do speaks so loud that I cannot hear what you say.

— Ralph Waldo Emerson

The most important thing in communication is hearing what isn't said.

— Peter F. Drucker

While language is the key to the heart of a culture, nonverbal communication is the heartbeat of a culture.

— Ting-Toomey

PART ❶ Warm Up

1. Watch a video clip to get some ideas about nonverbal communication.
2. Look at the following gestures and try to guess their meanings.

(1)   (2)   (3)   (4)

(The pictures are adopted from http://image. baidu.com)

PART ❷ Readings

Passage 1 The Basics of Nonverbal Communication

The following is what most scholars agree on, about nonverbal communication, in terms of its definitions, importance, and functions.

Defining Nonverbal Communication

The study of nonverbal communication has only a relatively short history. In the early 1920s, a book titled *Physics and Character* was published and this is supposed to be the first book on nonverbal communication. Then in 1952, another book titled *An Introduction to Kinesics* was published, which is regarded as a classic book on nonverbal communication. And then in 1959, Edward T Hall published his important book *Silent Language*. These books have laid foundation for nonverbal communication. Here are some of the most widely accepted definitions of nonverbal communication:

- Metacommunication, paralinguistics, second-order messages, the silent language, and the hidden dimension of communication.   —— Hall, 1959

- all those messages that people exchange beyond the words themselves.

—— Judee K. Burgoon, 1996

- all nonverbal stimuli in a communication setting that is generated by both the source and his or her use of the environment and that has potential message value for the source or receiver.   —— L. A. Samovar & R. E. Porter, 2004

Samovar and Porter's definition not only marks the boundaries of nonverbal communication, but also reflects how the process actually works. This definition permits us to include intentional and unintentional behavior in the total communication event. That is to say, sometimes nonverbal is intentional, as with the use of gesture such as the thumbs-up sign to indicate that we approve. Sometimes it is unintentional, sometimes embarrassingly so, as when we blush. We send countless messages that we never intend to be part of the transaction.

Definitions of nonverbal communication differ from one expert to another. Simply, nonverbal communication refers to communication without the use of words.

The Importance of Nonverbal Communication

Researchers have shown that the words a person speaks may be far less important than the body language used when delivering the verbal message. They estimate that less than 30% of communication between two individuals within the same culture is verbal in nature. Over 70% of communication takes place nonverbally. Some other scholars even say that 90% of the information is actually transmitted through nonverbal means. We are not sure of that. But one thing we are sure about is that in face-to-face communication nonverbal signals are just as important as verbal message.

Nonverbal communication is important because we use the actions of others to learn about their affective or emotional states. Research indicates that sometimes nonverbal signals play a more decisive role than verbal messages in determining communicative effects. For instance, whether what you say is a joke or an insult depends on the facial expression and tone that accompany what you say. It's often not what you say that counts but what you don't say.

Nonverbal communication is significant in human interaction because it is usually responsible for first impressions. Think for a moment of how often your first judgments are based on nonverbal messages. More importantly, those initial messages usually color the perception of everything else that follows. Even how we select friends and partners is grounded in first impressions, just as a Chinese saying goes, "Fall in love at first sight."

Nonverbal communication has value in human interaction because many of our nonverbal actions are not easily controlled consciously. This means that they are relatively free of distortions and deception.

Nonverbal communication is also important to the study of intercultural communication because a great deal of nonverbal behavior speaks a universal language. People tend to have similar meanings for behaviors such as smiling, frowning, laughing, and crying. In such a situation as international business, when people are not from the same speech community, nonverbal cues will be even more heavily relied on. Nonverbal communication can often be your only first-hand knowledge of a foreign colleague who speaks a language you don't understand. Even if you know the language, cultures differ in the use of nonverbal communication. Costly business blunders are often the result of a lack of knowledge of another culture's oral and nonverbal communication patterns. And misunderstandings can be harder to clear up because people may not be aware of the nonverbal cues that led them to assume that they aren't liked, respected, or approved. The literature is filled with scenarios of how misreading of nonverbal cues leads directly to cross-cultural friction.

The need to master the knowledge of nonverbal behavior in another culture increases the challenge of working successfully in an international business setting. Therefore, successful communication in the international business environment requires not only an understanding of language but also the nonverbal aspects of communication that are part of any speech community.

Functions of Nonverbal Communication

Nonverbal communication has its own unique functions in interpersonal communication. We will sum up some of the important ways that nonverbal communication regulates human interaction.

Replacing [1] . It can replace verbal communication, as with the use of

Notes
[1] 代替

gesture. Suppose someone asks you a question. Instead of answering verbally, you nod your head vertically — up and down. By doing so, you replace the action meaning "yes" for the word "yes." If a group of people is noisy, you might place your index finger to your lips as an alternative to say, "Please calm down so that I can speak."

Regulating [2] . We often regulate and manage communication by using some form of nonverbal behavior. For example, we have direct eye contact with someone to let him or her know the channels are open. Turn taking (i.e. who speaks first and for how long) is largely governed by nonverbal signals.

Conveying [3] . Nonverbal behavior conveys our emotions and our attitudes toward ourselves and toward the people we are communicating with. For example, the phrase, "I would love to meet with you and discuss this issue in more details," can convey different meanings and attitudes depending on the nonverbal signals accompanying the words.

Modifying [4] . Nonverbal communication can modify verbal communication. Loudness and tone of voice can be an example here. You can accent your anger by speaking in a voice that is much louder than the one you use in normal conversation.

Repeating [5] . People often use nonverbal messages to repeat a point they are trying to make. We might hold up our hand in the gesture that signifies a person to stop at the same time we actually use the word "stop."

Complementing [6] . Closely related to repeating is complementing. For example, you can tell someone that you are pleased with his or her performance, but this message takes in extra meaning if you pat the person on the shoulder at the same time. Physical contact places another layer of meaning on what is being said.

Contradicting [7] . On some occasions, our nonverbal actions send signals opposite from the literal meanings contained in our verbal messages. For example, you tell someone you are relaxed and at ease, yet your voice quavers and your hands shake. People rely mostly on nonverbal messages when they receive conflicting data like these, so we need to be aware of the dangers.

(Adapted from "Intercultural Business Communication" by Dou Weilin)

Notes

② 控制
③ 表达或传达（思想、感情等）
④ 改善
⑤ 重复
⑥ 补充
⑦ 矛盾

Questions

1. What is nonverbal communication?
2. Why is nonverbal communication so important in intercultural communication?
3. When contradictory messages are sent through both verbal and nonverbal channels, which channel do you think is more accurate? Why?

Passage 2 ▶ Kinesics and Proxemics

We send and receive nonverbal messages every day because nonverbal communication exists regardless of whether or not we speak. Without being able to use words, our bodies generally express our feelings and attitudes. In other words, we are communicating nonverbally either consciously or unconsciously almost at any time.

The elements of nonverbal messages include hand gestures, eye contact, posture and stance, facial expressions, odors, clothing, hairstyle, walking behavior, interpersonal distance, touching, architecture, artifacts, vocal signs, color symbolism, cosmetics, timing and pose, and silence. For the purpose of study, we classify these elements into four categories: kinesics ①, proxemics ②, paralanguage, and chronemics. Here are the first two categories and the other two are discussed in the next passage.

Kinesics

Kinesics is the study of body movements and activities in human communication. It is also called body language. The four most common body activities are: facial expressions, eye contact, hand gestures, and touch.

Facial Expressions

Facial expressions are the most obvious and important source of nonverbal communication. The Chinese people have always said that a person's character is clearly written on his or her face. This belief is reflected in Chinese operas in which face paintings are used to indicate the personalities and dispositions of the characters. In communication we constantly observe

Notes

① 体势语（该学科研究人的身体语言，如姿势、手势、体态、动作及面部表情等对交际的影响）

② 空间关系学（该学科研究人与人在不同社会环境中或不同社会团体或文化群落之间对空间的需要以及人对周围空间的感觉）

and interpret the meanings of expressions from faces of others. The six basic human emotions can be easily reflected on our faces: surprise, fear, anger, disgust, happiness, and sadness.

Across cultures, the same facial expression may acquire different meanings. For example, we tend to consider smiling as a universal nonverbal cue that symbolizes a happy feeling. In Japan, however, smiling serves another purpose. To the Japanese, the smile not only expresses happiness and affection but is also a way to avoid embarrassment and unpleasantness. For example, the Japanese always smile at the guests no matter how sad the situation is, even when the friends come to see the last face of one's deceased husband.

Eye Contact

The way we use eye contact not only transmits [3] messages to others and reflects our personality but also indicates what we are thinking about. For example, research shows that when we move our eyes up and to the left we are recalling something we have seen before, and when we move our eyes up and to the right, we try to envision something we never saw before.

The use of eye contact follows some unstated rules. For example, staring at a person at a distance may mean an invitation for interaction, and returning of the gaze is generally interpreted as acceptance of the invitation. In addition, more mutual eye contact appears among friends than others, and persons seeking eye contact while speaking tend to be more believable. However, these rules may vary in different cultures. Cross-culturally, the misinterpretation of the use of eye contact can lead to serious misunderstanding. For example, in North America it is impolite for a man to gaze at women, but Italian men may gaze at women all the time and the women don't feel offended. People in the Middle East, especially Arabs, also consider gazing a way to show respect in communication, because they think one can see a person's soul from the person's eyes. This is why political leaders from that area often wear sun eyeglasses when they are interviewed by reporters. It is difficult to hide information if the reporters can see their eyes directly.

Hand Gestures

Humans are superior to other animals not only because we are capable of using hands to handle tools but also because we can use hand gestures as symbols in communication. We use a wide range of hand gestures to "talk"

Notes
③ 传递

with each other in daily communication.

Most hand gestures are culturally determined. For example, the ring sign with index finger and thumb in a circle means "Okay" to Americans and money to the Japanese. Moreover, to the French the ring sign indicates that we think someone is a "zero," and to people in Malta it is an invitation to those who have homosexual inclination. And hand gestures are often used in social greetings. For instance, Westerners shake hands; Tanzanians clap hands ten times to say hello; the Polish and Romanians kiss the back of the hand; Eskimos use hands to give a friendly punch on the head or shoulder; Thais and Indians put hands together in front of the face and slightly bow.

Touch

Touch, or haptics [4], refers to how we use touch in the process of communication. Touch that can be defined as communication include handshakes, holding hands, kissing (cheek, lips, hand), back slapping, high five, a pat on the shoulder, and brushing an arm.

All cultures have rules dealing with who, how, why, when, and under what circumstances people may engage in physical contact. Public or private touching (or its absence) communicates an enormous amount of information, beginning with how you greet someone (handshake, kiss(es) on the cheek, embrace, bow, etc.), continuing throughout a conversation to the leave-taking and conclusion of a meeting. The meaning conveyed from touch is highly dependent upon the context of the situation, the relationship between communicators, and the manner of touch.

In addition to facial expressions, eye contact, hand gestures, and touch, kinesics includes many other elements such as body movement or posture, hairstyle, clothing, and artifacts. Artifacts are things like cosmetics, jewelry, bandages, ribbons, tattoos [5], glasses, and hair ornaments that we use to adorn ourselves and that can send messages to others. Yawning can transmit the message that we are tired or not interested in a topic. Clothing can communicate our emotion and behavior and can also differentiate us from other people and designate whether a situation is formal or informal. Lastly, people of different cultures show diverse ways of using body movement or posture. For example, squatting is popular in Japan, India and China, but is viewed as childish, primitive, and uncomfortable by Northern Americans.

Notes
[4] 触觉
[5] 刺在皮肤上的图案

Proxemics

Proxemics refers to the study of how human beings and animals use space in the communication process. The language of space is powerful. How close can we get to people? How distant should we be? Most of us never think about the space; we intuitively know what the right distance is. Our use of space in communication is an excellent illustration that culture is learned and not inborn. Though our parents may have given us some verbal instruction on space, we have learned most of our behavior by means of observation. We simply do what is "right." Arabs learn the same way, and so do Japanese, Mexicans, Russians, and the members of all other cultures. The problem is that the acceptable use of space varies widely among cultures. What feels right for us may be totally offensive to someone else. Space in many ways becomes an extension of us, and we feel uncomfortable with people who play by different rules.

Private Space

Our private space is sacred, and we feel violated if someone invades that personal bubble. In the United States that bubble is about the length of an arm, and people talk about keeping relationship at arm's-length to mean that they want to keep someone at a distance and not allow that person into their personal sphere. That bubble is a little bit smaller in France, but larger in the Netherlands and Germany. It is even larger in Japan but much smaller in Latin countries and the Middle East. The size of the private space is also influenced by social status, gender, age and level of authority, further complicating the interpretation of space in communication.

Our attitudes toward space reflect our attitudes toward privacy. Northern Europeans cherish their privacy and arrange their dwellings accordingly. Property boundaries are marked carefully, and everyone ensures that they are not violated. Fences and hedges separate gardens. Traditionally, a German house had a fence around the front yard with a gate that was closed and in many cases locked. In contrast to Germany, houses in the United States may have fences and hedges surrounding the backyard, but the front yards are wide open and inviting. Doors tend to be open for an invitation to come in. If someone tends to be alone, the door may be closed.

In Japan privacy is defined altogether differently than it is in the United States and Germany. Japan is a crowded country, and space is costly; therefore, houses and apartments are smaller. Walls and doors are thin, traditionally made of wood and parchment paper. Sound carries easily. Yet within this crowdedness the Japanese are able to create a private sphere. The private bubble and the personal space are more a creation of the mind than an actual space. Americans connect privacy with physical space, whereas Japanese people connect privacy with mental space.

Public Space

The way people arrange and use public space also reflects cultural attitudes toward space and privacy. Two people from different cultures may look at the same space yet come to entirely different conclusions.

People from the United States carry their idea of individuality over into public spaces. They consider it their right to walk and play on the grass in the park. After all, it is their park; their taxes paid for it. Government buildings in the United States are open to the public. Anyone can go into the Capitol in Washington or the various state capitols. In no other country is the residence of the president open to the public.

The Germans organize their public spaces in the same way they organize their private lives. Order is an overriding[6] concern, and detailed provisions are made to guarantee that order. Germans tend to not have problems with this control because they grew up with an emphasis on order. As a result, parks tend to be clean and neat; the grass is not trampled upon. This order is achieved through the use of numerous signs; "It is forbidden to step on the grass" is typical and is enforced.

Generally, people from Northern Europe prefer a larger physical space and therefore stand farther apart in waiting lines. People from Latin American countries, in contrast, have a smaller physical space and stand closer. Seeing space in lines at EuroDisney, Latin American visitors frequently try to fill in the space left by people from Northern Europe. This annoys the Northern Europeans.

As above mentioned, differences in using space often cause misunderstanding in intercultural communication. North Americans may feel that Arabs from North Africa and from the northern and western Middle

Notes
[6] 最主要的

East intrude on their personal space. Likewise, Arabs complain that North Americans have an aloof or indifferent attitude in communication. The way we approach people and the way we deal with space and issues of privacy have deep cultural roots. We may not agree with or like what others do. That is not the issue; the point is that we must understand what the others are doing and why they are doing it.

(Adapted from "Foundations of International Communication" by Guo-Ming Chen & William J. Starosta, and from "Intercultural Communication in the Global Workplace" by Iris Varner & Linda Beamer)

Questions

1. Do you think the message sent nonverbally to be explicit or implicit? Why?
2. How do you categorize nonverbal communication?
3. What do we study with kinesics and proxemics?
4. Could you cite some examples to show how the use of space varies widely between cultures?

Passage 3 ▶ Paralanguage and Chronemics

Aside from kinesics and proxemics as two of the most important categories of nonverbal communication discussed in the previous passage, there are two more types of nonverbal communication that play essential roles in people's daily life, that is, paralanguage and chronemics ①. In the following paragraphs, more information about these two categories is provided.

Paralanguage ②

Paralanguage refers to the study of voice or the use of vocal signs in communication. Comprised of all the sounds we produce with our voices that are not words, paralanguage forms the border between verbal and nonverbal communication. Vocal cues can be used to detect the emotional state of the speaker in communication. They not only reflect the degree of liking communicated but also suggest the personality of the speaker. For example, we tend to think that persons are more dynamic if they increase the rate,

Notes

① 时间学（跨文化交际中对时间的研究）

② 辅助语言，也指狭义的副语言（研究发声系统的各个要素，如音质、音幅、音调、音色等对交际的影响）

loudness, and pitch of their speech. We also tend to think the persons are more persuasive if they are more fluent in their speeches, using more volume, higher speech rates, and more intonation. According to Trager, paralinguistic cues can be classified into four categories: voice qualities[3], vocal characterizers[4], vocal qualifiers[5], and vocal segregates[6].

Voice quality consists of the recognizable characteristics of our voice that are separated from the actual messages. These paralinguistic cues include pitch range, quality of articulation, rhythm, resonance, and pace. Each individual has a distinctive voice quality. A person's voice may be muffled, childish, or nasal, and another's can be breathy, resonant, or melodious. For example, North Americans tend to think a woman is discontent when she uses a strident and high-pitched voice, and sexy when she uses a breathy and low-pitched voice. In Japan men are considered to be more masculine or authoritarian when they use a low-pitched voice with great volume.

Vocal characterizers are nonverbal voices that reveal our physical and emotional state. It is nearly universal for humans to laugh when they are happy; cry when they are in sorrow; yell (or to be totally silent) when they are angry at someone; and yawn when they are tired. Vocal characterizers also include cues such as belching, groaning, hiccupping, moaning, sighing, sneezing, snoring, and spitting.

Vocal qualifiers are variations of our voice that convey our emotions and personality. They represent the range of volume from soft to loud, low to high pitch, and the extent of our word elongation[7]. In other words, they include the manner in which a word or phrase is uttered — the changes of volume, pitch, and the speech rate used in communication. Every language system possesses its own acceptable range of vocal qualifiers. For example, in the Arab world speaking loudly signifies being strong and sincere, but such behavior may seem irritating and aggressive to North Americans. Vocal qualifiers are also reflected in the international community. For example, foreign students from different cultures show a distinctive variation in speaking English in the United States. The variations often become a source of distancing when the local population evaluates such differences negatively.

Vocal segregates are those voice noises that seem not to serve any function but to interfere with the flow of speech. Examples include "um,"

Notes
③ 音质（指辅助语言中，说话人声音的基本特质）
④ 嗓音特征表露（指在辅助语言里，人通过发出如笑或哭这类声音来"说话"）
⑤ 语音修饰（指辅助语言里，根据强度修饰话语而产生短暂延音的声音）
⑥ 发声间隔（指在辅助语言里，发生类似于语言的声音，但它不出现在可被严格地称为言辞的序列里）
⑦ 延伸

"uh," "eh," "I mean," and "you know" in the middle of speaking. Like that of vocal characterizers, the use of vocal segregates is fairly universal. However, the duration, placement, and use of vocal segregates may vary in different cultures. For example, within the Aristotelian rhetorical tradition, Westerners feel it more appropriate to decrease the use of vocal segregates in a speech or conversation, whereas in China their use signals wisdom and attractiveness.

Chronemics

Chronemics is the study of how we use time in communication. There are two ways to study the concept of time. First, we can look at time or a continuum connecting it into the past, the present, and the future. Second, we can classify it into monochronic time and polychronic time.

Past, Present, and Future Time Orientation

Past-oriented cultures emphasize tradition and history. People having this orientation evaluate daily or business plans based on the degree to which their plans fit with customs and traditions. Innovation and change tend to be discouraged. When change is necessary, it should be justified by the past experience. China is an example of a past-oriented culture. Historical dramas in television series or movies often produce high box office sales in Chinese societies. Also in Saudi Arabia, any person who "changes" is presumed to be violating Muslim religion.

Present-oriented cultures consider the present as the only precious moment: Seize the day! We should enjoy today and not worry about what may happen tomorrow. Similarly, the "Protestant ethic" advocates, "work for the night cometh." The bus schedules in the Bahamas illustrate a present-time orientation. There the individual drivers set arrival and departure times, taking breaks whenever they feel like it. For example, if a driver feels hungry, he or she may go home directly to have lunch.

In contrast, future-oriented cultures emphasize planning in order to achieve goals. Changes and innovations are encouraged in those cultures and are evaluated in terms of future economic payoffs. The United States tends to be present- and near-future-oriented. For instance, in business Americans may have 5- or 10-year plans, but in practice they evaluate the employee's performance on a monthly or quarterly basis. A manager may be fired because of poor performance at the end of the first quarter. The Japanese are future-oriented people, as clearly shown by their system of life-long employment.

Monochronic and Polychronic Time Orientation

According to Hall, monochronic-time-oriented cultures tend to treat time as something fixed in nature. Time is like the air surrounding us, which we cannot escape. Thus, time is linear, segmented, and manageable. People in monochronic-time-oriented cultures tend to do one thing at a time and to follow precise scheduling. In social interactions, making appointments and meeting deadlines are common practice. Austria, Germany, Switzerland, and the United States are some examples of monochronic-time-oriented cultures.

Polychronic-time-oriented cultures do not emphasize scheduling by separating time into discrete, fixed segments. Instead, they treat time as a less tangible medium in which many things can be done simultaneously. Thus, in these cultures, personal interaction and relationship development are far more important than making appointments or meeting deadlines. Africans, Arabs, Greeks, Mexicans, Native Hawaiians, Portuguese, and Spanish are generally included in this category. Misunderstandings or conflicts may occur between people from monochronic- and polychronic-time-oriented cultures, as Hall vividly described in 1984, explaining the tendency to view the "different" as "annoying" or "wrong:"

"Particularly distressing to Americans is the way in which appointments are handled by polychronic people. Being on time simply doesn't mean the same thing as it does in the United States. Matters in a polychronic culture seem to be in a constant state of flux. Nothing is solid or firm, particularly plans for the future; even important plans may be changed right up to the minute of execution."

In 1992, Victor summarized the characteristics of monochronic and polychronic time orientations. According to Victor, in monochronic time-oriented cultures, preset schedules dominate interpersonal relations; appointment times are rigid; people handle one task at a time; breaks and personal time dominate personal ties; time is inflexible and tangible; personal time and work time are clearly separated; organizational tasks are measured by activities per hour or minute. In contrast, in polychronic time-oriented cultures, interpersonal relations supersede [8] preset schedules; appointment time is flexible; people handle many tasks simultaneously; personal ties

Notes
[8] 取代

dominate breaks and personal time; time is flexible and fluid; personal time and work time are not clearly separated; and organizational tasks are measured as part of the overall organizational goal.

(Adapted from "Foundations of International Communication" by Guo-Ming Chen & William J. Starosta, and from "Intercultural Communication in the Global Workplace" by Iris Varner & Linda Beamer)

Questions

1. What do we study with paralanguage and chronemics?
2. Are paralinguistic cues significant in provoking expected effects of a speech? How do we use them to help deliver a successful speech?
3. Could you offer examples to illustrate the differences between monochronic-time-oriented cultures and polychronic-time-oriented cultures?

PART ❸ Exercises

Section A Culture Quiz

1. **Watch a video clip and try to identify the 10 surprising ways which may offend people from the different cultures.**
2. **Interpret the following nonverbal actions from the perspective of your culture.**
    1) An elderly woman dresses entirely in black.
    2) A young man dresses entirely in black.
    3) An adult pats a child's head.
    4) A student in the school dining hall waves his hand over his head and snaps his fingers loudly.
    5) Two men kiss in public.
    6) Two young ladies walk hand in hand in the street.

Section B ▶ Group Discussion

Read the following passage and discuss how to prepare for a job interview nonverbally.

Candidates often spend several hours preparing for interviews, particularly at the executive level, where they are expected to enter meetings with a solid understanding of the business, the industry, and the position. Unfortunately, all of this hard work can be undermined if the applicant fails to pay attention to the manner in which he or she is communicating.

Here are eight common interview pitfalls with advice for how to avoid them:

◇ A weak handshake. Right or wrong, many hiring managers believe if your handshake is weak, so is your personality. A firm, quick grip conveys self-confidence and professionalism.

◇ Avoiding eye contact. While it is tempting to admire the view outside the office window, use eye contact when speaking. Guard against staring by occasionally redirecting your glance.

◇ Crossing your arms. Intentional or not, this tells interviewers you are on the defensive — and it may have the same effect on them. Keep your arms open and to the side, or loosely fold your hands in your lap.

◇ Invading the interviewer's space. Leaning forward in your seat, for example, may be moving out of the comfort zone between you and the interviewer. It is important to sit upright, but relaxed, in your chair.

◇ Making tense facial expressions. It has been said it takes 43 muscles to frown. Try to sense when your facial muscles are tightening and smile when appropriate.

◇ Nodding persistently. Nod as a natural response when you strongly agree on ideas or opinions that have been presented.

◇ Overusing hand motions. While gestures can help emphasize important points, too much movement is distracting.

◇ Tapping your fingers or feet. You might have a nervous habit, but these actions will give the impression you are anxious to end the interview. Instead, focus your energy on the conversation.

Section C ▷ Intercultural Practice

Suppose you are Professor Wang, a consultant working at a cross-cultural organization, which provides help and offers suggestions to those who feel puzzled at some cross-cultural problems. The following are some e-mails you received last week. Reply to each of them with some explanations and constructive suggestions.

E-mail 1

Dear Professor Wang,

One night my friend Maria and I were getting ready to go out for the evening. Before we could leave, Maria had to call her friend Rodrigo to come and pick us up because Maria did not have a car. I was nervous because I had not yet met Rodrigo.

I had borrowed Maria's clothes and earrings so I would fit into the foreign style. Rodrigo finally arrived around midnight. Maria introduced us, and I, being culturally sensitive, remembered I had to kiss Rodrigo on the cheek instead of shaking his hand. I kissed Rodrigo once on each cheek. After the greeting Rodrigo gave me a strange look and glanced at my left hand. Maria started to laugh as Rodrigo remained puzzled and asked me why I was not wearing my wedding ring.

I really want to know: Why had Rodrigo thought I was married?

Sincerely,

Jessica

E-mail 2

Dear Professor Wang,

My name is Linda, and I am an 18-year-old American girl. I decided to study abroad in China. I am also a very affectionate person. When I arrived in China, I gave big hugs to all the members in my travel group. When we went to meet our instructors, I spontaneously gave them all a warm hug. After that first meeting with my instructors, I found that their attitudes toward me had changed. Each time I saw my instructors, I found them to be very distant and cold toward me. Could you explain what happened and why?

Sincerely,

Linda

E-mail 3

Dear Professor Wang,

I was sitting in the London underground one day, minding my own business, reading a magazine, while waiting for the train to arrive. All of a sudden I looked up and saw a British man staring at me. He was standing to the right of me, about one foot away and could not take his eyes off me. My initial reaction was to just ignore him, so I looked up at him, smiled, and then continued to read my magazine. No longer than two seconds later, I heard him say, "You're American, aren't you?" I immediately responded by saying, "Yes, how did you know?"

How could a stranger know that I'm from the States?

Warmest regards!

Daisy

E-mail 4

Dear Professor Wang,

My uncle went for a summer holiday to Bulgaria. There he had difficulty finding a parking space for his car. He finally found an empty area but there weren't any signs indicating parking was not allowed. So he asked a passer-by and he just nodded. So my uncle parked his car and went shopping. Later, when he came back to the car he noticed that he was fined with a parking ticket under the windscreen wipers. What happened?

Sincerely,

David

Section D ▶ Case Studies

Case 1

"Is He Sure?" I'm Not Sure

Rana Zari from Lebanon has been working for a Swedish firm for several months. When she arrived in January, she did not think she would last very long; the short days and the cold winter made her wonder how anyone could live in such an environment. But now that summer has arrived, she is getting used to the climate and her surroundings. She likes her work, and her colleagues are friendly, but she doesn't have a real feeling for them. What do they think? How do they live? What do they do in their free time? What are their hobbies? In her previous job in Beirut, for example, she would socialize with her co-workers after hours.

She knew about their families, and in the office there was an easygoing camaraderie (同志间的友谊和忠诚). Rana misses the enthusiastic greetings with co-workers and the hugs with the other female employees. In Stockholm her co-workers are friendly but more distant. Rana is used to speaking with her whole body, using her arms to emphasize her points, and showing her emotions through her facial expressions. Increasingly she is wondering how she is doing. Her boss, Arne Gustafson, seems to appreciate her work, but sometimes she has doubts. He never just comes out and says, "Great job!" Yesterday he called her into his office to set the agenda of an upcoming negotiation session with managers from Malaysia. Rana knows that the firm faces tough competition and a joint venture with the Malaysia firm would help open the Asian market. Arne discussed the negotiation strategy and gave her several assignments for the negotiation. He was all business, objective but without emotion. Rana is wondering: Is he confident that this Malaysian negotiation will go well? Does he have any doubts? What does he think is going to happen? Is she doing her part? His words sound confident, but during her time in Sweden she has found that she has not been very successful at reading the thoughts and emotions of her co-workers.

(Adapted from "Intercultural Communication in the Global Workplace" by Iris Varner & L.

Beame)

Question

Why couldn't Rana feel certain about what her colleagues and boss were thinking about?

Case 2

Monochronic Americans and Polychronic Mexicans

A large American telecommunication company introduced a technically superior product on the world market. It planned to focus specifically on increasing sales in Latin America, where it had not been very successful previously. The only serious competitor was a French company which had an inferior product, but whose after-sale support was reputedly superior.

The Americans went to great pains to prepare their first presentation in Mexico. "Judgment Day" would begin with a video presentation of the company and its growth potential in the medium-long term. After this, vice-president of the group would personally give a presentation to the Mexican minister of communications. Also meticulously planned was the two-hour lunch. Knowing Mexican culture, they believed this was where the battle would be fought. The afternoon session was reserved for questions and answers. The company jet would then be ready to leave Mexico City in the last departure "slot." It was tight, efficient and appreciated, right?

Wrong, the Mexican team threw off the schedule right away by arriving one hour late. Then, just as the Americans were introducing the agenda for the day, the minister was called out of the room for an urgent phone call. He returned a while later to find that the meeting had gone on without him. The Mexicans were upset that the presentation had proceeded, that the after-sales service contract was separate from the sales contract and that the presentation focused only on the first two years after installation rather than the long-term future together.

The French, on the other hand, prepared a loosely structured agenda. They determined some of the main goals to be attained by the end of the two-week visit. The timing, the where and the how were dependent on factors beyond their control, so they left them open. A long presentation on the historical background of the French state-owned company was prepared for the minister and his team. It had done business with Mexico's telephone system as early as 1930 and wanted to re-establish a historic partnership. As far as the French were concerned, the after-sale service, which extended indefinitely, was part of the contract. It was the French who received the order for a product known in the industry to be technologically less sophisticated.

(Adapted from "Riding the Waves of Culture" by Trompenaars & Turner)

Question

Why did this large American telecommunication company which can provide a technically superior product fail to sign the contract in Mexico?

Case 3

Flirting with Disaster

Mark had recently migrated from Denmark to Sydney, working as a salesperson for a large Australian company. After three weeks, he was invited to join a local club, and Mark was excited by his admission to the club. During the first few weeks of the club's activities, Mark was either standing in a corner talking with someone or sitting in a sofa listening to other people chatting. As time went by, he came to know most of the club members and seemed to enjoy talking with them. One day at an evening party, one of the ladies came up and showed some interest in talking with him. As a matter of fact, that lady came to his attention the first time he was attending the club's activities, and her willingness to talk with him now was sort of cliff hanger. He immediately showed his eagerness to chat her up and they began talking about the atmosphere of the party before the lady began to ask him questions about his home country. At first, the talk between them seemed to be quite smooth, but as the talk went on, the lady seemed to step back again and again while Mark advanced, looking at her in an undefined way. The lady obviously seemed uncomfortable. Just when Mark was about to ask her questions about Australian social customs, another man standing by threw a glance at the lady and then, she excused herself and went to talk with that man, leaving Mark standing there alone and wondering why their talk came to such a sudden end.

(Adapted from "An Analytical Survey of Cultural Clashes" by Wang Fuxiang & Ma Dengge)

Question

Why did the lady turn a cold shoulder to Mark at the party?

PART ❹ Additional Reading

Do's and Taboos: Cultural Aspects of International Business

Understanding and heeding cultural variables is one of the most significant aspects of being successful in any international business endeavor. Some of the cultural distinctions that firms most often face include differences in business styles, attitudes toward development of business relationships, attitudes toward punctuality (准时), negotiating styles, and gift-giving customs regarding titles.

American firms must pay close attention to different styles of doing business and the degree of importance placed on developing business relationships. In some countries, business people have a very direct style, while in others they are much more subtle. Many nationalities value the personal relationship more than most American do in business. In these countries, long-term relationships based on trust are necessary for doing business.

Many U.S. firms make the mistake of rushing into business discussions and "coming too strong" instead of nurturing the relationship first. According to Roger Axtell in his book *Do's and Taboos of Hosting International Visitors*, "There is much more to business than just business in many parts of the world. Socializing, friendships, etiquette, grace, and patience are integral parts of business. Jumping right into business discussion before a get-acquainted interlude can be a bad mistake."

Building a personal rapport (关系) is also important when doing business in Greece, according to Sondra Snowdon, President of Snowdon's International Protocol, Inc., a firm that trains and prepares executives in cross-cultural communications. Business entertaining is usually done in the evening at a local tavern, and spouses are often included. The relaxed atmosphere is important to building a business relationship based on friendship. Belgians, however, are the opposite, Snowdon says. They are likely to get down to business right away and are usually conservative and efficient in their approach to business meetings.

Attitudes toward punctuality vary greatly from one culture to another. Romanians, Japanese, and Germans are very punctual, while many of the Latin countries have a more relaxed attitude toward time. The Japanese consider it rude to be late for a business meeting, but see it as acceptable, even fashionable, to be late for a social occasion. In Guatemala on the other hand, according to Ford, a luncheon at a specified time means that some guests might be 10 minutes early, while others may be 45 minutes late.

When crossing cultural lines something as simple as a greeting can be misunderstood. Lack of awareness concerning the country's accepted form of greeting can lead to awkward encounters. Traditional greetings may be a handshake, hug, nose rub, kiss, placing the hands in praying position, or various other gestures. But the form of greeting differs from culture to culture. For instance, the Japanese bow is one of the most well-known forms of greeting. The bow symbolizes respect and humility (谦逊) and is a very important custom to observe when doing business with Japanese. There are also different levels of bowing, each with a significant meaning, Japanese and Americans often combine a handshake with a bow so that each culture may show the other respect.

People around the world use body movements or gestures to convey specific message. Though countries sometimes use the same gestures, they often have very different meanings. Misunderstanding over gestures is a common occurrence in cross-cultural communication, and misinterpretation along these lines can lead to business complications and social embarrassment. As we've mentioned earlier, the "OK" sign commonly used in the United States is a good example of a gesture that has several different meanings according to the country. In France, it means zero; in Japan, it is a symbol for money; and in Brazil, it carries a vulgar connotation.

Proper use of names and titles is often a source of confusion in international business relations. In many countries (including the United Kingdom, France, and Denmark), it is appropriate to use titles until use of first names is suggested. First names are seldom used when doing business in Germany. Visiting business people should use the surname preceded by the title. Titles such as "Herr Direktor" are sometimes used to indicate prestige, status, and rank. Thais, on the other hand, address each other by first names and reserve last names for very formal occasions, or in writing. When using the first name they often use the honorific "Khun" or a title preceding it. In Belgium, it is important to address French-speaking business contacts as "Monsieur" or "Madame," while Dutch-speaking contacts should be addressed "Mr." or "Mrs." According to Sondra Snowdon, confusing the two is a great insult.

Customs concerning gift-giving are extremely important to understand. In some cultures, gifts are expected, and failure to present them is considered offensive. Business executives also need to know when to present gifts — whether or not on the initial visit; where to present gifts — in public or private; what type of gift to present; what color it should be ; and how many to present.

Gift-giving is an important part of doing business in Japan. Exchanging gifts symbolizes the depth and strength of a business relationship to the Japanese. Gifts are usually exchanged at the first meeting. When presented with a gift, companies are expected to respond by giving a gift. In sharp contrast, gifts are rarely exchanged in Germany and are usually not appropriate. Small gifts are fine, but expensive items are not a general practice.

Gift-giving is not a normal custom in Belgium or the United Kingdom either, although in both countries, flowers are a suitable gift if invited to someone's home. Even that is not as easy as it sounds. For example, avoid sending chrysanthemums (especially white) in Belgium and elsewhere in Europe since they are mainly used for funerals. In Europe, it is also considered bad luck to present an even number of flowers. Beware of white flowers in Japan where they are associated with death, and purple flowers in Mexico and Brazil that carry similar connotations.

These cultural variables are examples of the things that U.S. executives involved in international business must be aware of. At times in the past, Americans had a poor track record of being sensitive to cultural distinctions. However, as business has become more global, Americans have been more sensitive to cultural differences and the importance of dealing with them effectively. Still, some companies fail to do their homework and make fatal or near-fatal mistakes and have learned the hard way that successful domestic strategies do not necessarily work overseas and that business must be adapted to the culture. An American company ultimately must not only have a sensitivity to other cultures but also have a good understanding of its own culture and how other countries see American culture.

(Adapted from "Cultural Aspects of International business, Business America" by M. Katherine Glover)

Questions

1. What happens if a firm fails to take notice of the cultural differences in nonverbal communication?
2. Could you cite examples to show that attitudes toward punctuality vary from one culture to another?
3. Do the same gestures always entail the same meaning in different cultures? Give examples to explain why or why not.
4. Could you make some comments on the custom of gift-giving in China?

Cultural Values

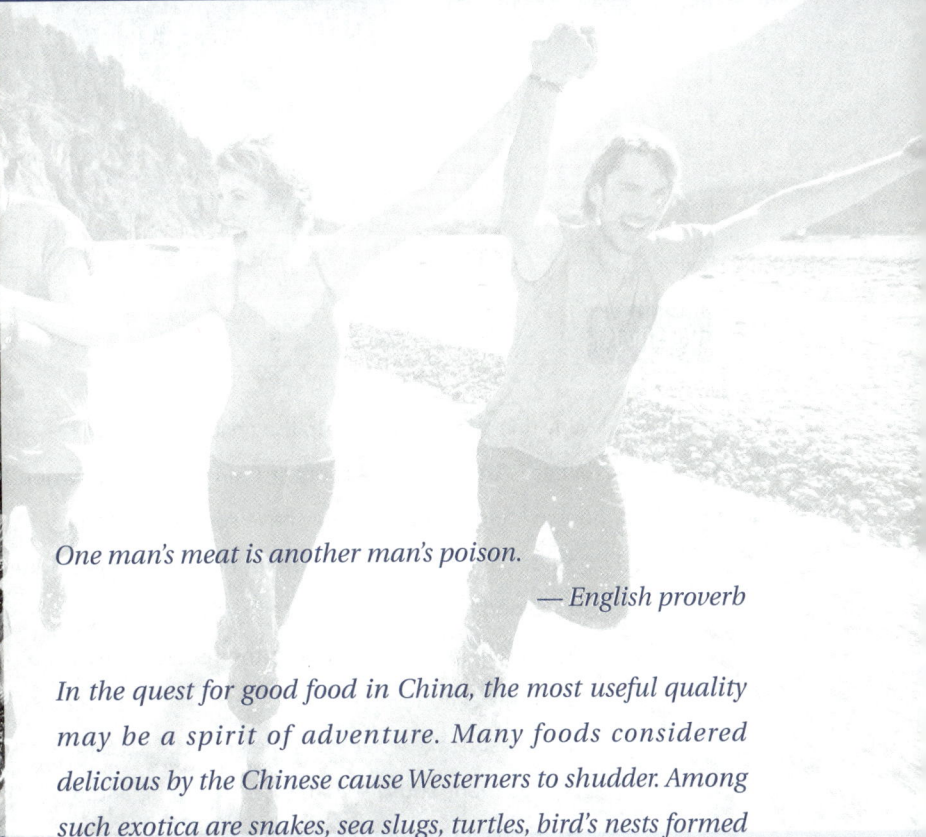

One man's meat is another man's poison.

— English proverb

In the quest for good food in China, the most useful quality may be a spirit of adventure. Many foods considered delicious by the Chinese cause Westerners to shudder. Among such exotica are snakes, sea slugs, turtles, bird's nests formed of swallows' saliva, dried jellyfish, and webs of duck feet.

— TIME, October 5, 1987

Your beliefs become your thoughts. Your thoughts become your words. Your words become your actions. Your actions become your habits. Your habits become your values. Your values become your destiny.

— Mahatma Gandhi

PART ❶ Warm Up

1. Watch a video clip about one of our Chinese cultural values to get some ideas about the concept of collectivism.

2. Look at the following picture and try to answer the questions below it.

Questions

1. Why don't the parents help the child to stand up?

2. What is the usual reaction of Chinese parents when their children fall down? And why would they have such a reaction?

3. Could you tell what values are reflected in the following proverbs?

    1) Blood is thicker than water.   (Scotland)

    2) God helps those who help themselves.   (Greece)

    3) Time is money.   (U.S.)

    4) The squeaky wheel gets the grease.   (U.S.)

    5) Too many cooks spoil the broth.   (England)

    6) However crowded the way be, the hen will reach her eggs.   (Africa)

    7) Haste makes waste.   (England)

    8) A man's home is his castle.   (England)

    9) Think three times before you take action.   (China)

    10) Modesty makes you progress, whereas conceitedness makes you lag behind.   (China)

    11) A single arrow is broken, but not in a bunch.   (Japan)

    12) Whoever teaches me a letter, I should become a slave to him forever.   (Egypt)

PART ❷ Readings

Passage ▶ 1 The Role of Values in Intercultural Communication

A concept becomes a value to a people when they consider it as extremely desirable or undesirable. Values are thus positive or negative on the same continuum ①: while one people might consider a concept as most desirable, another might say it is most undesirable, and a third might not have a reaction. The first group welcomes the value, the second avoids it, while the third does not care one way or the other. Members of the first group might speak out in favor of the concept or belief in question; they might even try to impose it on others. The second group would of course do everything possible to fight what they perceive as the negative value.

For our purpose, a value will be defined as follows:

Value seems to be the basis of all decisions that a person makes. It tells him how something ought to be and for what his life is worth living, worth fighting, and even worth dying. Since value is so important, it is also necessary to influence others to accept it as the only end state of life. Values thus become the standard for a person to judge his own and other's actions.

This definition underscores ② the importance of values in guiding human behavior toward oneself, toward others, and toward one's culture.

Discussion of values is not new. In the fourth century B.C., Aristotle mentioned the character of speaker or ethos ③ as an important value that affected communication. At about the same time, the Buddha talked about too much greed as a negative value, and Confucius said that authoritarianism ④ is necessary for the welfare of a society.

Values and Communication

Studies conducted on the role of values in human behavior have revealed a number of ways in which values and communication are related. Much of the existing research supports two general propositions about that relationship.

First, values are communicated, both explicitly ⑤ and implicitly ⑥, through symbolic behavior. Although what we say and what we do may reflect our personal motives or are constrained by the context of a situation, most of our speech and actions symbolically reflect the values embedded [7] in our mind that have been learned through the socialization process. Values are normally expressed through verbal and nonverbal behaviors. Verbal expressions are used to highlight the importance of specific values to individuals or groups. Proverbs demonstrate how verbal expressions are used to underscore values. For example, certain cultural values are expressed in the proverbs used by North Americans:

Time and action: "Time is money." "A stitch in time saves nine."

Practicality: "A bird in the hand is worth two in the bush." "Don't cry over the split milk." "Don't count your chickens before they are hatched."

Privacy: "A man's home is his castle."

Cleanliness: "Cleanliness is next to godliness."

Future orientation: "Take care of today, and tomorrow will take care of itself."

Nonverbally, we tend to communicate our values through social rituals. For example, the custom of exchanging gifts in China and Japan reflects the cultural values of reciprocity [8], generosity, and friendship.

Second, the way in which people communicate is influenced by the values they hold. Just as communication is a mediator of values, communication is shaped by our value system. Because values determine what is desirable and what is undesirable, they dictate the way we choose to act in the process of communication. For example, harmony as a key Chinese cultural value leads the Chinese to avoid saying "no," to speak admiringly and respectfully of others, and to avoid expressing aggressive behaviors in social interactions. In other words, the values we hold influence our preference in selecting communication channels and sources that symbolize our value system. Thus the relationship that exists between communication and values is both mutual and reciprocal [9].

Values and Intercultural Communication

Differences in values create gaps in communication and could even cause non-communication. Values, then, are the most important variables in intercultural communication. The problem that arises with the difference in values is that we tend to use our own values as the standard when judging

Notes

[7] 扎根于

[8] 互惠

[9] 互惠的

others. We tend to assume that our value system is the best, an assumption that causes us to make value judgments of others. Such an attitude is ethnocentrism [10] . A careful study of communication at interpersonal level as well as via the media shows that most communication is ethnocentric. Most news stories in today's newspaper on other cultures and countries are ethnocentric. Analyses of contents of newspapers around the world would certainly show ethnocentrism of their reporters and editors.

Ethnocentrism is not limited only to news stories on mass media. Even the lessons we teach in our schools and colleges are ethnocentric. We always imply that our culture and country are the greatest. While there is nothing wrong with being proud of our culture and country, it is not right to imply that others are inferior. Our textbooks in social sciences and humanities contain plenty of ethnocentric information. Even the references and bibliographies are works from our own culture and country. We ignore the works of others with the reason: "Other books are not very good."

What is solution to the problem of ethnocentrism? Is there any way we can communicate better interculturally? Herskovits, a famous scholar, suggests one solution. He says the opposite of ethnocentrism is cultural relativism. It is the study of the values of others within the framework of that culture rather than in comparison with our own values. It is not easy to practice cultural relativism. We are brought up in an ethnocentric world. The practice of cultural relativism should begin at a very early age. We have to teach our youngsters to practice it. They should learn that each value or custom is developed by its people to make their life easy and meaningful. Each value system is meant to establish order in its own society. Instead of doing "comparative studies" of others, we should study others as they are. Then, we need not look at other ways of speaking as "accent" and our way as standard speech.

Perhaps even cultural relativism is not the ultimate answer. Because each culture has something to offer to the world, it is necessary to locate that something in each culture. Effective communication is needed about what each culture can contribute to the rest of the world. That communication should be free of ethnocentrism as well as relativism. The communicator could be able to point out the best aspect of a culture so others could borrow it and enrich themselves. The purpose of intercultural communication should be to

Notes
[10] 民族文化中心
    主义

help each participant share his or her experience with another so each could enrich the lives of other persons. When sharing expands from the individual to the entire culture, then intercultural communication would have achieved the ultimate goal of all human interaction.

The Two Rules

When members of different value systems interact, such communication becomes intercultural. While it would not be hard for members of the same value system to understand each other's values, it may not be so for those of different systems. Therefore, the first rule of intercultural communication is that each participant should understand the other's values. That understanding should precede any attempts to communicate interculturally. Because communicative techniques are manifestations ① of one's own values, the participants communicate differently. The second rule is that each should adapt his or her communication to the other's values. Adaptation implies respect for the other's value system. Without such respect one can not adapt his or her communicative behavior to the other system. Adaptation should be an on-going act. A person should know the art of constant adaptation to other cultures.

(Adapted from "Handbook of Intercultural Communication" by M. K. Asante, E. Newmark & C. A. Blake, and from "Foundations of Intercultural Communication" by Guo-Ming Chen & W. J. Starosta)

Questions

1. How do values affect communication?
2. Could you cite examples to illustrate the term "ethnocentrism?" What is the solution to ethnocentrism?
3. When members of different value systems encounter, what should they do in order to achieve mutual understanding?
4. Would you first make a list of major Chinese traditional values and then think about the ones that have changed with the passage of time?

Passage 2 ▶ Patterns of Friendship

A student from Japan studying in America was being visited by her sister, and when they went to a department store, a clerk came over to them. "Hi" she said, "How are you today?" Surprised, the sister said: "Do you know her?" A student from Germany was confused that everyone she met in the U.S. was so nice and friendly to her right away. Americans are often found to be very friendly and helpful to people that they do not know very well, and they may also be more open in what they talk about than people from many other countries. This can be confusing to someone who comes from a country where people are initially more reserved [1]. An international student may also feel that Americans are superficial [2] or are not "good" friends when this initial friendliness does not continue into friendship.

Like other aspects of culture, friendship is perceived differently in various parts of the world. So in the following we are going to discuss friendship in the United States, compared to friendship in China, to illustrate how patterns of friendship can be different across cultures.

The word "friend" in the United States has a broad meaning, including everyone from a casual acquaintance [3] to a long-time best friend. Americans tend to use the word "friend" whereas people in some other countries might use the word "acquaintance," and they often have different types of friends: friends just to do activities with, close friends, and best friends. In some countries, however, people reserve the word "friend" for a few people whom they are very close to. The following chart describes some of these levels of friendship.

Notes
① （指人或性格）
矜持的
② 表面的
③ 泛泛之交

The Levels of Friendship

Term	Definition	Customary Behavior
Neighbor	Someone who lives next door, across the street, or in the same block.	Neighbors generally say hello when they see each other. Some become good friends. They often help each other, borrow things, and watch each other's houses when no one is at home.

Term	Definition	Customary Behavior
Acquaintance	Someone you have been introduced to but do not know well.	Acquaintances generally say hello when they meet and make small talks.
Best Friend	Someone you can rely on and would feel comfortable asking for assistance at any time.	Best friends generally share both their good and bad times together and spend much of their free time together.
Boyfriend/Girl-friend	Someone of the opposite sex for whom you have romantic feelings.	Go on dates, share displays of affection, and walk arm in arm in public.
Girl Friend	A female friend of another woman (men and boys do not refer to their male friends as boyfriends).	Spend some time together and share common interests.
Classmate	A student in your class.	Say hello, make small talks, and occasionally study together.
Business Associate or Colleague	Someone who works in the same place of business as you do.	Share business information, discuss problems related to work, and occasionally socialize.

Jia Yuxin, a famous scholar in China, compared the patterns of friendship between people in China and America, and found that the aim in setting up friendship, the involvement in the friendship and expectations of friends differed dramatically. The following is a chart revised after Jia's comparative description of their differences.

Chinese Friendships and American Friendships

Chinese Friendship	American Friendship
Affective	Instrumental
Friend in need	Fair weather friend
Totalization of a person	Compartmentalization[④] of a person
Deep commitment and obligation	No deep commitment or obligation
High degree of familiarity	Low degree of familiarity
Interdependence	Independence
Solid, stable and long-lasting	Vulnerable[⑤], unstable and short-lived
Small circles, few in number	Big circles, large in number
Centered around affectivity	Centered around activity
Friends of the same gender	Friends of both genders

Notes
④ 分类
⑤ 脆弱的

As seen above, the American pattern shows how Americans are initially very friendly and open. However, American values stress privacy and independence, and it is not easy for many people to move beyond initial friendliness into the stage of true friendship. Thus, many international students are very happy when the Americans they meet are so friendly and open. However, when Americans do not continue to act in a way that an international student expects of a friend, the international students are often disappointed and confused. They may sometimes conclude that Americans are superficial and do not really know how to be friends. What the international students may not realize is that they have not yet reached the stage of being good friends with the Americans: they need to go over some "higher walls" before reaching the center and a good friendship. Alternatively, Americans living in a country where people are more reserved and not as initially friendly as in the U.S., may sometimes become discouraged about ever making friends in that country: they may feel that people in their host country are being unfriendly.

Different ways of building and maintaining friendship lead to different expectations of a friend. A student from China said that her American friends got mad if she asked them to do too many things for her, so she always asked her Chinese friends for help. She said that in China, one puts the needs of friends before oneself. A student from Switzerland was asked if he and the American girl he was speaking to were friends. He said no, which insulted the girl, as she considered them to be friends. He told her that in Switzerland it took time to make friends, and that friendship really meant something.

Two important American values are privacy and independence. Thus, Americans prefer to do things by themselves rather than ask for help, as they do not want to impose on the other person's time and privacy. They may also expect others to do the same. This can create misunderstandings with people from societies with more interdependent relationships, who assume more obligations to friends.

(*Adapted from "Gateway to Intercultural Communication" by Song Li*)

Questions

1. Why do international students conclude that Americans are superficial and do not really know how to be friends?
2. How do Americans define friendship?
3. What does friendship mean to Chinese people? Could you offer some examples to illustrate your point of view?
4. Based on what you have learned, what tips could you give to those who want to make friends with Americans?

Passage 3 ▶ Family Structure

Family structure is the core of any culture. This unit probably varies more among cultures than any other social structure.

A major function of the family is to socialize new members of a culture. As children are raised in a family setting they learn to become members of the family as well as members of the larger culture. The family provides the model for other relationships in society. Through the observations and modeling of the behavior of other family members, children learn about the family and society including the values of the culture.

Family structure and its inherent ① relationships and obligations are a major source of cultural differences.

The family is the center of most traditional Asians. Many people worry about their families' welfare, reputation, and honor. Asian families are often extended, including several generations related by blood and marriage living in the same home. Misdeeds of an Asian person are blamed not only on the individual but also on the family — including the dead ancestors.

Traditional Chinese, like many other Asians, respect their elders and feel a deep sense of duty toward them. Children repay their parents' sacrifice by being successful and supporting them in their old age. This is accepted as a natural part of life in China. In contrast, taking care of one's aged parents is often viewed as a supererogatory ② responsibility in the United States, where family support is not uncommon but not regarded as a duty which parents do not expect their children to fulfill.

Filipinos are considered the most Americanized of the Asians, but they still remain extremely family-oriented. Filipino parents are dedicated to helping their children and will sacrifice greatly for their children to get an education. In turn, the children are devoted to their parents, who often live nearby. Grown children who go away and leave the country for economic reasons typically send significant portions of their salary home.

The Vietnamese family consists of people currently alive as well as the spirits of the dead and the unborn. Thus many Vietnamese believe that their actions in this life will influence their status in the next life. Any decisions or actions are made through considerations of the family, not individual priorities ③ . Individual's behavior is judged on whether it brings shame or pride to the family. Children are trained to rely on their families, to honor the elderly, and to fear foreigners.

In conventional Japanese family, fathers are often stern and aloof. Japanese college students in one study said they would tell their fathers just about as much as they would tell a total stranger. The emotional and communicational barrier between children and fathers in Japan appears very strong after children have reached a certain age.

Notes
① 内在的
② 职责以外的
③ 优先权

Traditional Latin Americans are generally as family-centered as the traditional Asians. The family is the central frame of reference and Latin Americans believe that family members must help one another. Children in Latin America (of whom there are many, due to high rates of fertility) are taught to respect authority which is often paternal and increases with age. The family in most parts of Latin America includes many relatives, who remain in close contact. Family connections are the main way to get things done. In fact, name dropping (mentioning the names of important people the family knows) is often necessary to accomplish even simple tasks.

Although "family values" are often mentioned in the United States, the family is not the only frame of reference for decisions in America. Often a person's own individual "track record" of personal achievements is a powerful predictor of future success.

Thus, many cultural differences exist in family structures and values. In some cultures, the family is the center of life and the main frame of reference for decisions. In other cultures, the individual, not the family, is primary. In some cultures, the family's reputation and honor depend on each person's actions; in other cultures, individuals can act without permanently affecting the family life. Some cultures value the elderly, while others do not show great respect for them.

(Adapted from "Intercultural Communication in English" by Xu Lisheng)

Questions

1. What cultural values are reflected in these different family structures?
2. In which way do American family values differ from those of Asian families?
3. Is your family similar to or different from traditional Chinese family? If it's different, can you describe some of the differences? What brought about those changes?

PART ❸   Exercises

Section A ▶ Culture Quiz

1. Watch the video *A Cultural Conflict — Personal Values* presented by Capilano University students and fill in the following chart accordingly.

Name	Personal Description	Core Value
Richard Egger	Always on time	Punctuality
Kelly Ngo	Hates waiting around	_____
Farzad Ahmri	Loves his family	_____
Josh Woodman	Hates missing Canucks games	_____
Sara Tayebi	A hard worker	_____

2. Look at the values on each side of the chart. Which value is the most important to you? Circle the number that most closely represents your point of view and you will see your own values.

1) It is important to maintain harmony (not to talk about subjects where there is disagreement).	1 2 3 4 5	It is important to talk about and resolve differences.
2) The needs of the group are more important than the needs of the individual.	1 2 3 4 5	The needs of the individual are more important than the needs of the group.
3) It is good to spend money now to get what is needed, so don't worry about tomorrow.	1 2 3 4 5	It is important to save money now, rather than spend it, so that there will be enough money in the future.
4) A person's importance is based on family or connection.	1 2 3 4 5	A person's importance is based on what he or she has done.
5) We should recognize and emphasize differences in power and status between people.	1 2 3 4 5	We shouldn't focus too much on power differences between people.

6) I prefer indirect communication.	1 2 3 4 5	I prefer direct communication.
7) I have flexible and open views about time, so we get there when we get there.	1 2 3 4 5	Being on time and keeping schedules is important.

(Adapted from "Tips for Teaching Culture: Practical Approaches to Intercultural Communication" by Ann C. Wintergerst & Joe McVeigh)

Section B▶ Group Discussion

"Face" refers to the public image of a person and plays a role when you communicate with others. "Face" is a very important concept in China. See how many phrases you can think of that contain the term "face." How important is "face" to you? Cite some examples in which "face" is concerned. What do you think "face" means? Why is "face" important in China? Do other nations have such a concept?

(Adapted from "Intercultural Communication" by Zhang Ailin)

Section C▶ Intercultural Practice

The following is a comparison between Americans and Chinese on the topic of happiness. Read it first and then work with your classmates to explain why there are similarities and differences between the two groups of students. Finally, think about what is happiness to you.

How Americans and Chinese Think About Happiness Differently

Researchers and thinkers have often claimed that cultures can be divided between individualistic cultures and collectivistic cultures. The former prioritize individual satisfaction and achievement, while the latter prioritize the collective goals of the family, group and society.

American and Chinese cultures are often seen as falling on the opposite ends of this spectrum. U.S. has gunslingers and cowboys, individual class mobility, i.e. the American dream, and Thoreau, who sat by a pond alone for two years. The Chinese have Confucian values, filial piety, guanxi ("relationships/networks"), and Yue Fei, the folk hero who tattooed "Serve the Country with Utmost Loyalty" on his back.

So how differently will individualistic cultures and collectivistic cultures answer the question: "What is happiness?" Two psychologists, Luo Lu and Robin Gilmour, asked 142 Taiwanese students and 97 Caucasian American students this exact same question. (Note the specific samples: The study didn't include mainland Chinese or non-white Americans, so the findings may not be definitely correct.)

Surprisingly, in general, the themes that emerged from the two groups were broadly similar. For example, in both groups, students described happiness as "mental states of satisfaction and contention," as "positive feelings/emotions," as "achievement," as "freedom from ill-being," and as "relating to people."

However, there were several points of difference between the Chinese students and the Caucasian American students. Here is the full list:

1) Chinese describe happiness as "Harmony" while Americans don't.

   While the Chinese students characterized happiness as a "harmonious homeostasis" (i.e., equilibrium or balance) within the self, as well as between the self and his environment; few American students referred to balance or harmony in their descriptions.

2) Americans focus externally while Chinese focus internally.

   The Caucasian American students gave individualistic descriptions of happiness focused on shaping the external world, such as self-autonomy, concrete achievement and positive self-evaluations. On the other hand, the Chinese students listed communal definitions of happiness focused on shaping the self, such as self-cultivation, mind-work and positive evaluations of the self by others.

3) Americans describe happiness as the "ultimate value" while Chinese don't.

   One unique theme found in the Caucasian American students' responses was happiness as the "ultimate value in life." Such strong emphasis placed on happiness was not found among the Chinese students, indicating that this may stem from an individualistic outlook, in contrast to a collectivistic outlook.

   Other empirical work supports this, finding that Chinese students placed less emphasis on happiness, and worried less than American students about whether they were satisfied with life.

4) Chinese focus on intense emotions less than Americans.

   As mentioned, researchers found broadly similar themes between Chinese and American students. Nonetheless, the details within these themes contained subtle differences. One important distinction is while both groups emphasized positive emotions, the Chinese students focus on intense emotions much less than the Caucasian American students.

5) Chinese and Americans perceive social relationships differently.

Another subtle difference can be found in the groups' perceptions of social relationships. Though both groups valued relationships, the Chinese students emphasized the merging of two selves to achieve interdependence, while the American students emphasized the negotiation of an accommodation between two people who remained independent.

6) Both believe happiness is up to yourself, but definitions of "autonomy" differ.

While both groups believed "we have personal responsibility for our happiness," they had differing definitions of self-autonomy. For the Americans, autonomy is ideally complete personal freedom to fulfill your potential and become your authentic self. For the Chinese, personal actions and choices must be governed by morality, and a meaningful life is a virtuous life. The Chinese students also believed that while a person should be autonomous, he or she must eventually accept what fate brings.

(Adapted from "How Americans and Chinese Think About Happiness Differently" by David Sze)

Section D▶ Case Studies

Case 1

"I hit him to show my respect for you!"

In the film *Gua Sha Treatment*, Datong is tidying up his desk in his office, preparing to quit his job because his boss and friend testified against him on behalf of his accuser, confirming that Datong hit his own son, Dennis, who offended the boss' son.

Datong: I don't want to talk to you.

Boss: Datong, I'm so very sorry. I'm trying to tell you…

Datong: I said I don't want to talk to YOU! Would you please give me a break?

Boss: I couldn't lie. They knew everything.

Datong: Leave me alone. I don't have the time or the intention to hear you justifying your action. I just want to get my son home to get my life back.

Boss: And that's why more than ever you need this job.

Datong: I considered you as my friend but you sold me out. How do you expect me to work with you again?

Boss: I just told the truth. You shouldn't have hit Dennis.

Datong: Why did I hit him? Why? My only son? I hit him to show my respect for you! To give you face, you know?

Boss: What kind of twisted Chinese logic is that? You have to hit your own son so that you can show respect for me?

Datong: 不可理喻。

Boss: What did you say?

Datong: Let me share this fine-known Chinese proverb with you: 道不同，不相与谋.

Questions

1. Why is Datong quitting his job? If you were Datong, would you do the same thing?

2. Why did the boss testify against Datong, his friend? Would you do the same or would you lie to help your friend?

3. Why did Datong hit his only son? Why didn't his boss understand his goodwill?

Case 2

Criticizing a Teacher

Shortly after Raymond started teaching English in an English training centre in China, the Director of the program called him to the office. The Director told him in a round-about way that the students were unhappy about some of his methods and had made some suggestions about his teaching. Raymond was embarrassed, not just because the students had concerns about his teaching style, but because the students had complained directly to the Director.

(Adapted from "Cultures in Contrast: Mis-Communication and Misunderstanding Between Chinese and North Americans" by Dai Fan, Stephen & L. J. Smith)

Questions

1. Why did the Chinese students complain directly to the Director?
2. What would American students do if they met the same problem?
3. If you were the Director, how would you explain the situation to Raymond?

Case 3

Does Family Come First?

Rosa (Mexican-American) and Annie (American) shared a small dormitory room at their university. They liked each other and got along until a problem came up.

One day, Rosa told Annie, "My second cousin wants to come and see the university. She might want to go to school here next year. Do you mind if she stays with us while she visits?"

"Gee, it's pretty crowded with just the two of us. Where's she going to sleep?"

"Oh, that's no problem. She can sleep in my bed, with me."

"Well, okay," said Annie. "It's up to you."

"Great!" answered Rosa. "She's coming tomorrow."

Two weeks later, the cousin was still with them. Since she did not bring enough money, Rosa paid for all her meals. Rosa missed many of her classes so that she could help her cousin find her way around.

Rosa never complained about any of this to Annie, but Annie decided to speak to her friend.

"Rosa," she said. "I know it's none of my business. But I don't like to see you being treated this way. It's not fair for your cousin to take advantage of you, using your time and money like this. And how do you ever get any sleep, anyway? I think you should tell her you have your own life to live. After all, she is only your second cousin."

Rosa was surprised. She answered, "Oh, the bed doesn't bother me! It reminds me of sleeping with my sister as a child. You are right, though, about my school work. I know I'm missing too many classes. But family comes first. I just couldn't leave my cousin here by herself."

Even after their conversation, Annie still could not understand her friend. Before her cousin arrived, Rosa had always seemed like such an independent, responsible person, who never missed a class. Annie just could not understand why she had changed.

(Adapted from "Intercultural Communication" by Zhang Ailing)

Questions

1. Why was Annie confused?
2. Why did Rosa continue to help her cousin?
3. What do you think of Rosa's and Annie's personal values?
4. Would you do the same for your relatives as Rosa did? Why or why not?

PART ❹   Additional Reading

Hofstede-Bond Research on Cultural Value Orientations

To study the relationship between cultural values and communication behaviors more systematically, Kluckhohn and Strodbeck in 1967 introduced the concept of value orientations. According to them, value orientations are the means society uses to solve the universal problems of daily life. The concept implies four assumptions. First, all human societies will face the same problems; second, they use different means to solve universal problems; third, the means to address universal problems are limited; and fourth, value orientations are behaviorally observable through empirical study. Cultural value orientations are often used to develop a cultural assimilator that enables people to understand their own and others' cultures in intercultural training programs.

Hofstede's Cultural Dimensions

During the 1980s, Hofstede compared work-related attitudes across over forty different cultures and found four consistent dimensions of cultural values held by over 160,000 managers and employees: individualism/collectivism (个体主义 / 集体主义), power distance (权力差距), uncertainty avoidance (回避不确定性), and masculinity/femininity (男性化 / 女性化). While Hofstede's work has been criticized for understating domestic cultural and gender variability, it offers a good starting point for thinking about values.

The dimension of individualism and collectivism describes the relationship between the individual and the group to which the person belongs. Individualistic cultures stress the self and personal achievement. People in an individualistic culture tend to emphasize their self-concept in terms of self-esteem, self-identity, self-awareness, self-image, and self-expression. In other words, the individual is treated as the most important element in any social setting. Personal goals supersede (取 代) group goals, and competition is often encouraged in this culture. Moreover, in individualistic cultures people tend to emphasize more affiliativeness (联系), dating, flirting, and small talk in social interactions. Hofstede's findings indicate that the United States, Australia, Great Britain, Canada, The Netherlands, New Zealand, Italy, Belgium, and Denmark all belong to this group.

By contrast, collectivistic cultures are characterized by a more rigid social framework in which self-concept plays a less significant role in social interactions. Ingroup (e.g., immediate and extended families) and outgroup members are clearly distinguished, and only ingroup views and needs are emphasized. In these cultures, people are also expected to be interdependent and show conformity (遵从) to the group's norms and values. In other words, the social networks are much more fixed and less reliant on individual initiative. Columbia, Venezuela, Pakistan, Peru, Chinese Taiwan, Thailand, Singapore, Chile, and Chinese Hong Kong are the top nine collectivistic cultures specified in Hofstede's studies. If we compare them with Hall's high- and low-context cultures, we can see that individualistic cultures tend to be similar to low-context cultures and collectivistic cultures to high-context cultures.

The dimension of power distance specifies to what extent a culture adapts to inequalities of power distribution in relationships and organizations. High-power-distance cultures tend to orient to authoritarianism, which dictates a hierarchical (等级制度的) or vertical structure of social relationships. In these cultures, people are assumed to be unequal and complementary in social interactions. The differences of age, sex, generation, and status are usually maximized. Thus, people in high-power-distance cultures develop relationships with others based on various levels of hierarchy. The Philippines, Mexico, Venezuela, India, Singapore, Brazil, Chinese Hong Kong, France, and Columbia represent the high-power-distance cultures in Hofstede's studies.

Low-power-distance cultures are more horizontal in terms of social relationships. People in these cultures tend to minimize differences of age, sex, statue, and roles. Instead, individual differences are encouraged. Australia, Israel, Denmark, New Zealand, Ireland, Sweden, Norway, Finland, and Switzerland are those countries that scored low in power distance scale.

The dimension of uncertainty avoidance measures the extent to which a culture can accept ambiguous situations and tolerate uncertainty about the future. Members of high-uncertainty-avoidance cultures always try to reduce the level of ambiguity and uncertainty in social and organizational life. They pursue job and life security, avoid risk taking, resist changes, fear failure, and seek behavioral rules that can be followed in interactions. As a result, high-uncertainty-avoidance cultures tend to use fewer oral cues and are more able to predict others' behaviors. Such cultures are found in Greece, Portugal, Belgium, Japan, Peru, France, Chile, Spain, and Argentina.

However, other cultures, including Denmark, Sweden, Norway, Finland, Ireland, Great Britain, the Netherlands, the Philippines, and the United States, are oriented to cope with the stress and anxiety caused by ambiguous and uncertain situations. Members of these low-uncertainty-avoidance cultures tend to better tolerate the deviant (反常的) behaviors and unusual stress connected with the uncertainty and ambiguity. As a result, they take more initiative, show greater flexibility, and feel more relaxed in interactions.

Finally, the dimension of masculinity and femininity refers to the extent to which stereotypically masculine and feminine traits prevail in the culture. In masculine cultures men are expected to be dominant in the society and to show quality of ambition, assertiveness (果断), achievement, strength, competitiveness, and material acquisition; thus, the communication styles are more aggressive. In male-dominant cultures women are expected to play the nurturing role. Hofstede's studies indicate that Japan is the best example of a masculine culture. Other nations in this category include Australia, Venezuela, Switzerland, Mexico, Ireland, Great Britain, and Germany.

Members of feminine cultures tend to emphasize the quality of affection, compassion, emotion, nurturing, and sensitivity. Men in these cultures are not expected to be assertive. Thus, gender roles are more equal and people are more capable of reading nonverbal cues and tolerating ambiguous situations. Sweden, Norway, the Netherlands, Denmark, Finland, Chile, Portugal, and Thailand represent feminine cultures, according to Hofstede.

Bond's Chinese Value Survey

Bond's study at the University of Hong Kong was much smaller, involving a survey of 100 (50% women) students from 22 countries and 5 continents. The survey instrument was the Chinese Value Survey (CVS), based on the Rokeach Value Survey. The CVS also tapped four cultural dimensions. Three corresponded to Hofstede's first, second and fourth ones. Hofstede's third cultural dimension, uncertainty avoidance, was not measured by the CVS. Instead, Bond's study isolated the fifth cultural dimension. It eventually was renamed *long-*

term versus short-term orientation to reflect how strongly a person believes in the long-term thinking promoted by the teachings of the Chinese philosopher Confucius. According to an update by Hofstede, "On the long-term side one finds values oriented toward the future, like thrifty (saving) and persistence. On the short-term side one finds values rather oriented toward the past and present, like respect for tradition and fulfilling social obligations." Importantly, one may embrace Confucian long-term values without knowing a thing about Confucius.

By merging the two studies of Hofstede and Bond, a serious flaw in each was corrected. Namely, Hofstede's study had an inherent Anglo-European bias, and Bond's study had a built-in Asian bias. How would cultures be compared if viewed through the overlapping lenses of the two studies? Hofstede and Bond were able to answer that question because 18 countries in Bond's study overlapped the countries in Hofstede's sample. Lists show the countries or regions scoring highest on each of the five cultural dimensions (countries earning between 67 and 100 points on a 0 to 100 relative ranking scale qualified as "high" in the following table). In terms of individualism, the United States ranks number one. So it is a highly individualistic society. But it scored moderate in power distance, masculinity, and uncertainty avoidance, and scored low in long-term orientation. Japan scored the highest both in masculinity and uncertainty avoidance, and scored higher in long-term orientation. So Japan is a highly masculine society. Men dominate in society, while women assume a much less dominant role. They are expected to look after their husbands and children. Hong Kong (China) scored the highest in long-term orientation.

Key Cultural Dimensions in the Hofstede-Bond Research
(Country or Region Scoring the Highest)

Individualism vs. Collectivism	Loose or tight social bonds? (U.S.)
Power distance	Expected social inequality? (Philippines)
Uncertainty avoidance	Preference for structured or unstructured situations? (Greece)
Masculinity vs. Femininity	Expression of competitive or nurturing traits? (Japan)
Long-term orientation vs. Short-term orientation (Confucian values)	Save for the future and be persistent or "live for today?" (Hong Kong, China)

(Adapted from "Foundations of Intercultural Communication" by Guo-Ming Chen & W. J. Starosta, and from "Intercultural Business Communication" by Dou Weilin)

Questions

1. Could you think about some differences between Chinese and Western cultures and use the five-dimension model to explain them?

2. Could you please make a small survey among students of different nationalities to prove this model?

Culture Shock

No people come into possession of a culture without having paid a heavy price for it.

— James A. Baldwin

It's incredible, but I think for a lot of people it shot over their heads because they're used to just getting images and messing around with them, and for us to do something quite so "designed" was a bit of a shock.

— Sean Booth

PART ❶ Warm Up

1. Watch a video clip about one of our Chinese cultural values to get some ideas about culture shock.
2. Read the following story and answer the questions below it.

Once in America I took a bus for an international conference. At the bus stop an old lady got on. Noticing there was no vacant seat on the bus, I decided to offer my seat to the old lady. I stood up and said to her: "Please sit down, old lady." Out of my expectation, the old lady refused to take the seat and responded: "I'm not old." There was also an unpleasant look on her face. I was rather confused and embarrassed at that moment, and didn't know what to do.

Questions

1. If you were sitting on a bus and then an old lady got on without any other vacant seat around, would you offer your seat to the old lady or refuse to give up your seat to her? Why?
2. Would you explain the reason why the old lady refused to take the seat on the bus?

PART ❷ Readings

Passage 1 ▶ What Is Culture Shock

Culture shock is a multifaceted① experience resulting from numerous stressors occurring in contact with a different culture. Culture shock occurs for immigrant groups (e.g., foreign students and refugees, businessmen on overseas assignments, etc.) as well as for Euro-Americans in their own culture

Notes
① 多层面的

and society (e.g., business institutions undergoing reorganization, populations undergoing massive technological and social change, and staff, clients, and public in schools, hospitals, and other institutions).

Culture shock is normal in a foreign culture environment, although those experiencing it may not recognize it or respond effectively to the problems. Effectively dealing with culture shock requires recognition of culture shock occurrences and implementing behaviors to overcome culture shock with stable adaptations. Awareness of the nature of culture shock and the typical reactions fosters constructive intervention by providing the basis for recognizing one's own ongoing culture shock experiences and for reframing the situations with adaptive responses and problem-solving strategies.

Phases or Stages of Culture Shock

The stages of culture shock and its resolution have been differentiated in a variety of ways, typically emphasizing four phases or stages. Underlying the different labels, the four primary phases of culture shock are typically considered to involve the following:

1. The honeymoon or tourist phase
2. The crises or culture shock phase
3. The adjustment, reorientation, and gradual recovery phase
4. The adaptation, resolution, or acculturation phase

The honeymoon or tourist phase. The first phase is the typical experience of people who enter other cultures for honeymoons, vacations, or brief business trips. It is characterized by interest, excitement, euphoria[2], sleeplessness, positive expectations, and idealizations about the new culture. The differences are exciting and interesting. Although there may be anxiety and stress, these tend to be interpreted positively. This is the opposite of what we think of as culture shock. This is because honeymooners, vacationers, and business people have experiences largely limited to institutions (hotels, resorts, business, and airports) that isolate them from having to deal with the local culture in a substantial way and on its own terms.

The crises or culture shock phase. When the honeymoon phase gives way to crises depends on individual characteristics, preparation, and many other factors. The crises phase may emerge immediately upon arrival or be delayed

Notes
② 愉快和兴奋的感觉

Notes

③ 关注

④ （指疾病）由精
神压力引起的，
因有精神压力而
恶化的

⑤ （似）偏执狂或
妄想狂的

⑥ 飞地（较大区域
内的小块不同民
族或人群的聚居
地）

but generally emerges within a few weeks to a month. It may start with a crisis or as a series of problems, negative experiences, and reactions. Culture shock may start immediately for some individuals. Although individual reactions vary, there are typical features of culture shock. Things start to go wrong, minor issues become major problems, and cultural differences become irritating. Excessive preoccupation③ with cleanliness of food, drinking water, bedding, and surroundings begins. One experiences increasing disappointment, frustration, impatience, and tension. Life does not make sense and one may feel helpless, confused, disliked by others, or treated like a child. A sense of lack of control of one's life may lead to depression, isolation, anger, or hostility. Excessive emotional strain and fatigue may be accompanied by physical or psychosomatic④ illness. Feeling as if one is being taken advantage of or being cheated is typical. Becoming overly sensitive, suspicious, and paranoid⑤ with fears of being robbed or assaulted are also typical reactions. One finds innumerable reasons to dislike and to criticize the culture. Plans for learning the language may be postponed, problems escalate, and depression may become serious. One generally wants to go home.

The adjustment, reorientation, and gradual recovery phase. The third phase is concerned with learning how to adjust effectively to the new cultural environment. Resolution of culture shock lies in learning how to make an acceptable adaptation to the new culture. A variety of adjustments will be achieved during cyclical and individually unique adjustment phases. There may be an adjustment without adaptation, such as flight or isolation. Many people who go to foreign countries do not adjust to achieve effective adaptation; instead, they opt to return home during the crises phase. Others use various forms of isolation, for example, living in an ethnic enclave⑥ and avoiding substantial learning about the new culture, a typical lifetime reaction of many first-generation immigrants. If one desires to function effectively, however, then it is necessary to adjust and adapt. One develops problem-solving skills for dealing with the culture and begins to accept the culture's ways with a positive attitude. The culture begins to make sense, and negative reactions and responses to the culture are reduced as one recognizes that problems are due to the inability to understand, accept, and adapt. An appreciation of the other culture begins to emerge and learning about it becomes an enjoyable challenge. During the adjustment phase the problems do not end, but one develops a positive attitude toward meeting the challenge of resolving the issues necessary to function in the new culture. Adjustment is slow, involving recurrent crises and readjustments.

The adaptation, resolution, or acculturation phase. The fourth stage is achieved as one develops stable adaptations in being successful at resolving problems and managing the new culture. There are many different adaptation options, especially given diverse individual characteristics and goals. Although full assimilation[7] is difficult if not impossible, one will acculturate[8] and may undergo substantial personal change through cultural adaptation and development of a bicultural identity. It is important to recognize and accept the fact that an effective adaptation will necessarily change one, leading to the development of a bicultural identity and the integration of new cultural aspects into one's previous self-concept. Reaching this stage requires a constructive response to culture shock with effective means of adaptation.

Causes of Culture Shock

Stress reactions. Exposure to a new environment causes stress. A normal consequence of living in and adjusting to a new culture is the experience of stress, which in turn increases feelings of anxiety, depression, uneasiness, and so on. Culture shock results in an increased concern with illness, a sense of feeling physically ill, a preoccupation with symptoms, minor pains, and discomforts, and may increase illness from stress-induced reductions in immune system functioning.

Cognitive fatigue. A major aspect of culture shock and the resultant stress is cognitive fatigue, a consequence of an "information overload." The new culture demands a conscious effort to understand things processed unconsciously in one's own culture. Efforts must be made to interpret new language meanings and new nonverbal, behavioral, contextual, and social communications. The change from a normally automatic, unconscious, effortless functioning within one's own culture to the conscious effort and attention required to understand all this new information is very fatiguing and results in a mental and emotional fatigue or burnout. It may be manifested in tension, headaches, and a desire to isolate oneself from social contact.

Notes
⑦ 同化
⑧ 适应文化

Role shock. Roles central to one's identity may be lost in the new culture. Changes in social roles and interpersonal relations affect well-being and self-concept, resulting in "role shock." One's identity is maintained in part by social roles that contribute to well-being through structuring social interaction. In the new cultural setting, prior roles are largely eliminated and replaced with unfamiliar ones and expectations. This leads to role shock resulting from an ambiguity about one's social position, the loss of normal social relations and roles, and new roles inconsistent with previous self-concept. For instance, dependence relations may no longer be supported, or conversely, a previously independent person may have to accept a dependent relationship with an authority figure.

Personal shock. This includes loss of personal intimacy and loss of interpersonal contact with significant others. One's psychological disposition, self-esteem, identity, feelings of well-being, and satisfaction with life are all created within and maintained by one's cultural system. The major and severe symptoms of culture shock may include withdrawal and excessive sleeping, compulsive eating and drinking, excessive irritability and hostility, marital and family tensions and conflicts, loss of work effectiveness, and unaccountable episodes of crying. Although these symptoms can characterize a variety of other maladies, if "the symptoms manifest themselves while one is living and working abroad, one can be sure that culture shock has set in." Personal shock is increased by occurrences in the new culture that violate one's personal and cultural sense of basic morals, values, logic, and beliefs about normality and civility. Value conflicts contribute to a sense of disorientation[9] and unreality, increasing the sense of pervasive conflict with one's surroundings.

(Adapted from "Cultural Shock and Adaptation" by Michael Winkelman)

Notes
[9] 迷惑；迷失方向

Questions

1. What do you think of the definition of culture shock? What kind of people may encounter culture shock?

2. What are the four stages of culture shock? Describe the characteristics of each stage.

3. What factors may contribute to culture shock?

Passage 2 Symptoms and Effects of Culture Shock

What symptoms of culture shock do people have when they sojourn in a foreign country? And what effects does culture shock bring about upon them? This passage discusses these questions in detail.

Symptoms of Culture Shock

The reaction to culture shock differs greatly from person to person. For some, it may take only a few weeks to work through the psychological distress due to the cultural difference they experience; for others, it may take a long period of time to overcome the frustration of culture shock. In very serious cases, the only way to eliminate the problem caused by culture shock may be a return to familiar surroundings.

As early as in 1985, Thomas stated that the symptoms of culture shock include depression, helplessness, hostility to the host country, feelings of anxiety, overidentification[1] with the home country, feelings of withdrawal, homesickness, loneliness, paranoid feelings, preoccupation with cleanliness, irritability, confusion, disorientation, isolation, tension, need to establish continuity, defensiveness, intolerance of ambiguity, and impatience. Oberg in 1960 vividly described the symptoms of culture shock as follows:

Excessive washing of the hands; excessive concern over drinking water, food, dishes, and bedding; fear of physical contact with attendants or servants; an absent-minded, faraway stare; a feeling of helplessness and a desire for dependence on long-term residents of one's own nationality; fits of anger over delays and other minor frustration; delay and outright refusal to learn the language of the host country; excessive fear of being cheated, robbed, or injured; great concern over minor pains and eruptions of the skin; and finally, a longing to be back home, to be able to have a good cup of coffee and a piece of apple pie, to walk into a fast-food restaurant, to visit one's relatives, and in general, to talk to people who really make sense.

Notes
[1] 过度认同

Effects of Culture Shock

As a transient experience, culture shock can be viewed as a transitional process of movement in which sojourners gradually become aware of and begin to adjust to cultural differences in a new environment. This process may proceed in one of the two directions, depending on individual personality.

In a positive sense, culture shock may contribute to individual growth. Adler in 1987 also pointed out culture shock may promote several beneficial outcomes for sojourners. First, culture shock provides a learning opportunity that demands new responses from sojourners in coping with a constantly changing environment. Second, because most people have a tendency to pursue unique and special goals, culture shock can create an environment and serve a motivational force for us to move to new levels of self-actualization[2].

Third, culture shock can give sojourners a welcome sense of challenge and achievement as a result of dealing with people from different backgrounds. Fourth, the amount of learning increases when the level of personal anxiety is aroused to a certain degree. To most of us, culture shock offers us a high but not extreme level of anxiety that causes us to learn about a new culture and about ourselves.

Fifth, the experience from culture shock produces new ideas that, in turn, offer us a new set of behavioral responses for future unfamiliar situations. Our sojourn strengthens us in the future by teaching us how to learn from negative cultural feedback. Finally, the new ideas we acquire during our sojourn mostly result from drawing comparisons and contrasts. This practice helps us to deal with cultures that we have not yet experienced.

Culture shock may also lead to negative consequences. First, culture shock constitutes a disorienting experience. On one day, we may experience feelings of mania[3] and excitement, while, on another, we may feel hysteria[4], confusion, anxiety, and depression. This uncertainty may be detrimental[5] to the psychological growth of some sojourners. Second, cognitively and perceptually, a set of desirable or proper behaviors in one culture might be considered bizarre or idiosyncratic[6] in another. Sorting through feelings about cultural differences may take a long time or may prove impossible for some. As a result, we may become prone to judge the unfamiliar more harshly than we

Notes
[2] 自我实现
[3] 狂热
[4] 歇斯底里
[5] 不利的
[6] 怪异的

did before our sojourn.

*(Adapted from "Foundations of Intercultural Communication" by Guo-
Ming Chen & W. J. Starosta)*

Passage 3 ▶ Constructing Adaptive Cultural Transformation Competence

Adaptive cultural transformation refers to a process in which one constantly adjusts one's own cultural beliefs, values, and behaviors to those in the target culture, and gradually develops multiple identities necessary to operate in different intercultural communication settings with appropriate, effective, and meaningful communicative performance.

Adaptive cultural transformation competence encompasses a wide array of competencies. It not only addresses what competencies one needs in successful communication, but also why and how such competencies can mark one's identities in different social settings. Adaptive cultural transformation competence can be referred to as the ability that enables an individual to communicate appropriately and effectively in the target culture by expanding his or her social identity to one that blends the new set of values, habits, and social norms in the target culture with those in the home country. It consists of a set of skills that are needed in appropriate, effective, and satisfactory cultural adaptation. Therefore, the adaptive cultural transformation competence model consists of three major components: social identity negotiation skills, culture-sensitive knowledge and mindful reflexivity, and communicative competence.

My adaptive cultural transformation in the U.S. did not come easily. The biggest challenge I have encountered in this process was how to strike a balance between my Asian cultural background and the American environment I was in, and between my identity in Chinese communities and in American communities. I was highly motivated to adapt myself to the American culture—to gain new cultural experiences in order to understand and appreciate the target culture. But my Chinese-self, characterized by Asian beliefs, values, customs, and habits often presented conflicts in the process of my adaptive cultural transformation, which required determination and willingness to recognize my own culture and to understand and respect the target culture.

In North America, I am regarded as a visible minority due to my Asian appearance. In order to maintain my L2^{①} social identity, i.e., to be accepted as a member of the target culture, which was a very important factor to the success of my professional career, I made extra efforts to improve my communication skills and mannerism in communication encounters. Due to my cultural adaptation, I am often taken or mistaken for a Chinese American. While being identified as a Chinese American can be a symbol of success of acculturation, it is not necessarily so within the Chinese community. I found it hard to be Americanized when I was with my Chinese friends. For instance, in an only-Chinese group, speaking English would be regarded as odd or showing off; likewise, dressing like Americans would be thought of as being alienated from the Chinese inner group.

Sometimes, I preferred to reveal my Chinese ethnic identity among American friends, or mixed groups when talking about something I was very proud of, such as Chinese ethnic food which I knew how to cook from home, and China's long history with numerous dynasties. Sometimes, I preferred to conceal my Chinese ethnic identity when the topic under discussion was something for which China was often being criticized, like its treatment of dissidents^{②}, and the bureaucracy of the government.

While I believe that personal preference of social identity is dependent on the social context, I strongly hold that my social identity has multiple dimensions. Each has its function when it's operated in the right context. I present myself as a different person in different social groups and communities. I was very quiet in class when I was in China as a sign to show respect to teachers, but I was very outspoken in class at Ohio State University (OSU) as a sign of cooperation with my teachers. I was not very talkative in Chinese communities in the U.S. as I did not want to show off, but I was very enthusiastic when talking about China and Chinese people among American friends as I considered myself a cultural informant. I seldom wrote Chinese letters to my relatives and friends in China, and I was not afraid of losing my Chinese, but I wrote almost every day in English as I still saw the weaknesses of my English writing. Therefore, I have to maintain different identities in different contexts and to vary my communication styles depending on when and where to speak what to whom.

I also find that social identity sometimes requires mutual acceptance. Even if I want to be affiliated with an ethnic group, I might be rejected. In order to understand American culture, I would spend Christmas Eve at my American friends' houses for years in a row③ even though I was invited again and again by my Chinese friends to go to their Chinese Christmas parties. One Christmas, when I wanted to be with my Chinese friends for a change, I was unfortunately not invited. I was told later by my Chinese friends that they thought I would have declined their invitation had they asked me again. I felt miserable about this experience. But perhaps my friends were right; affiliation to a certain ethnic group is reciprocal. What you want to be identified as is not enough without considering what others might think of you.

In my journey of adaptive cultural transformation, I gradually perceived my Chinese culture boundaries as permeable④ and flexible. Instead of letting my Chinese culture and my well-established first language social identity become a shield blocking me from constructing my second language identity in American culture, I became open-minded, and was willing to participate in various social activities to give myself opportunities to experience and understand the target culture. I was considered a fluent English speaker by many native English speakers in the U.S. But in my first quarter at OSU, I was so afraid of speaking up in the courses I took. I was overwhelmed by the various teaching styles professors used in different courses, the intensity of information given in each class, the amount of reading needed before each class, the weekly testing-format, and the outspokenness of my American classmates. As a result, I kept quiet, trying to figure out what I should do to carve a niche⑤ for myself in the new classroom culture. I conducted

Notes
③ 连续地
④ 有渗透性的
⑤ 占有一席之地

numerous "experiments" on myself in adapting to this special social setting — the academic content classroom. I tried to speak up when I was very sure of something, but failed the first few times, as I was nervous about making grammar mistakes. Then I tried several times to focus on the basic concepts in the readings and gave my interpretations of the concepts when they were discussed in class. Sure enough, my purposeful preparation somewhat helped my participation, but I still felt nervous to speak up in class as I could notice slightly unnatural tones in my voice. However, I kept trying and reflecting on my own experiences in participation and interaction with classmates. A couple of quarters later I realized that my participation in classes had become instantaneous[6], improvised[7], and effortless.

Learning some of the "normal" behaviors in classroom communication in the target culture, and unlearning some of the "normal" classroom behaviors in my own culture gradually brought about an internal transformation in me. In time, I deviated from the accepted patterns of my original culture in classrooms and acquired the new patterns of the target classroom culture. This led to an increased functional fitness, a greater congruence[8] and compatibility[9] between my internal state and the conditions of the American classroom environment. As a result, my increased oral participation in content courses[10] gradually made me aware of my existence in class. I could hear my voice in discussion, and I had a sense of belonging. This increased confidence in myself also gradually enabled me to attain a level of communicative success beyond the classroom setting to meet my social needs in such things as making friends with people from different cultural backgrounds, and seeking graduate research and teaching assistantships across campus. I gradually achieved psychological balance in terms of having high self-confidence, low level of stress and anxiety, and high self-esteem, as well as philosophical drives[11] in terms of being more creative in work and study, and having a sense of personal fulfillment.

While my increased classroom participation enhanced my functional fitness and the potential effectiveness of my communicative competence and performance in the target culture outside the classrooms, it has also affected my personality and self-identification, which changed from being mono-cultural to being increasingly intercultural. Instead of binding my group membership to the Chinese culture, I have taken a more fluid intercultural

Notes
[6] 即时的
[7] 即席的
[8] 适合；一致
[9] 和谐共存
[10] 基于内容的课程
[11] 豁达的魄力

identity by observing and practicing different sets of social values, beliefs, and norms in different cultural communities. Such an intercultural identity allows me to adapt to the situation and to creatively manage or avoid conflicts that occur frequently in intercultural communication settings. It is through this dynamic and continuous process of cultural adaptive transformation that my internal condition has gradually moved toward becoming increasingly intercultural.

(Adapted from "From an EFL Learner to an ESL Leader: Reflections in a Nonnative Voice" by Liu Jun)

Questions

1. Do you agree with the author that social identity is dependent on the social context? Why or why not?
2. Why was it hard to be Americanized when the author was with his Chinese friends?
3. What are the major differences between a traditional Chinese classroom and a typical American one?
4. What do you think Chinese students should do in order to adapt well to an American classroom?

PART ❸   Exercises

Section A   Culture Quiz

What would happen when people moved from one culture to another? When an individual enters an alien culture, he or she is like a fish out of water. Now please answer the questions by reading the picture below.

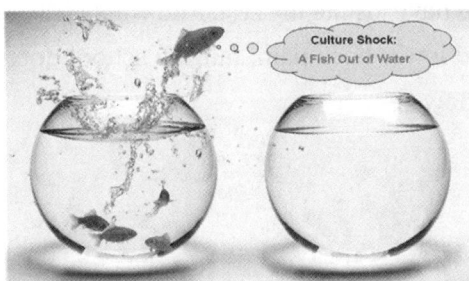

(The picture is adopted from https://www.moveoneinc. com/blog/wp-content/uploads/2011/08/moving- house-relocation-culture-shock.jpg)

Section B ▶ Group Discussion

The following are some excerpts from the e-mails of international students studying in Beijing. Please identify their stages of culture shock and explain their typical symptoms in group work.

E-mail 1

Dear Mom and Dad,

I'm feeling much better these days. Life here seems not so bad after all. The people are quite nice once you get to know them a little better and begin to figure out their way of looking at things. Guess what's new with me. I've just joined a running club in our university. Every afternoon around 4 o'clock, we meet on the campus playground and run together for an hour. Talking with those who share mutual hobbies with me is really fun. I also begin to try some local food there. Actually, the taste is not so bad, although I still feel like Mum's homemade apple pie.

Love,

Kim

E-mail 2

Dear Kelvin,

I'm really feeling fed up with my life here and longing for home. Getting anything done over here is a nightmare — the locals are so lazy and unhelpful. And on top of all that, I feel rundown and sleepy all the time, and seem to have lost all my zest. And worse still, I always feel an upset stomach, severe headache, and lower back pain, but the school doctor is of little help. I wish I could be back home right now.

Affectionate,

William

E-mail 3

Dear Nicole,

This is a fantastic place! So many interesting things to see, such as the Forbidden City and the Temple of Heaven. Even wandering the streets is a delight with all the bustle and hordes of cyclists. I'm really happy I came. The roasted duck here is so delicious that I could not imagine how I could endure turkey for so many years!

Best regards!

George

E-mail 4

Dear Wendy,

Thanks for your letter. It was lovely to hear from you. I've been thinking about your question about what I find the strangest about living in China — but the trouble is that I've been here so long and have settled into the way of life so much that everything seems perfectly ordinary! So, if you want to find out, you'll have to come out to see for yourself with a fresh pair of eyes. I can be your guide!

Warmest regards!

Pauline

Section C ▶ Intercultural Practice

Work in pairs, preparing for a mini-role-play. One has just come back from Japan, talking about his exciting experience of eating bugs in Japan where it has become a recent fashion as a green diet, while the other is from the Untied States where eating bugs is considered as disgusting and barbaric. Try to put on a short play to show the culture shock induced by the different food customs.

1: Are they delicious, noodles with bugs?   2: Do you like it, nicely decorated sushi?

(The pictures are adopted from www.ln.xinhuanet.com)

Section D▶ Case Studies

Case 1

An American Traveling Abroad

When I first visited Italy, I had taken a semester of beginning Italian before my departure to have some basic Italian survival skills. I felt quite confident with my limited Italian ability. Little did I know that upon arriving in Rome, I'd be completely lost. What I thought would be a pleasant visit turned into a nightmare! I was unable to communicate with anyone. I couldn't even get on a bus. It was embarrassing! I was on my own in a country with a language in which I could not even communicate. After the first week and multiple attempts to shop for groceries, find restaurants, and visit tourist sites, I finally relaxed and convinced myself that if I did get lost, someone would help me get back to my apartment. After I changed my attitude, I was able to deal with my daily chores and enjoy the next part of my Italian adventure.

(Adapted from "Tips for Teaching Culture: Practical Approaches to Intercultural Communication" by Ann C. Wintergerst & Joe McVeigh)

Questions

1. Why was the author unable to enjoy her first week in Italy even though she had learned some basic Italian survival skills?
2. How did she cope with culture shock and finally enjoyed herself?
3. Do you like traveling abroad by yourself? What can you learn from this case?

Case 2

Homesickness

Huang was the first born son of a well-to-do family in Hong Kong. He had done well in his undergraduate studies at the University of Hong Kong and had been accepted for graduate studies at a prestigious American university. He made his initial adjustment fairly well, finding housing and joining a support group made up of other students from Hong Kong who lived near his university. After a time, however, he began to be disappointed in his work and was unhappy with life in America. He liked an American woman, but the relationship broke up because of their differences in personality. While not failing any of his classes, he was by no means among the top students in his department, as shown by both test scores and participation in class seminars. Not wanting his friends from Hong Kong to learn about his problems, Huang went to the student health center with complaints about an upset stomach, severe headaches, and lower back pain. The doctor at the health center prescribed acetaminophen with codeine. Huang began to take the pills, but the problem persisted.

(Adapted from "Intercultural Interaction: A Practical Guide" by R. Brislin, K. Cushener, C.
Cherrie & M. Yong)

Question

Could you help explain what's happening to Huang?

Case 3

My Mother is Ill

In a police office in Hong Kong, a Chinese policeman (A) comes up to his British superior (B).

A: Sir.

B: Yes. What is it?

A: My mother is not very well, sir.

B: So?

A: She has to go to hospital, sir.

B: Well, get on with it. What do you want?

A: On Thursday, sir.

B: Bloody hell, man. What do you want?

A: Nothing, sir.

Questions

1. Can you guess why the policeman goes to his superior's office?
2. What do you think has caused the misunderstanding?
3. What should the Chinese policeman say to get what he wants?

PART ❹ Additional Reading

Why Is Reverse Culture Shock Worse than Culture Shock

Surveys of sojourners preparing to return home show that most anticipate little or no difficulty in readapting to their native culture. However, most will actually experience more stress during reentry than during their entry into another culture. Those who adjusted best and were the most successful overseas usually experience the greatest amount of difficulty with reverse culture shock.

A host of factors help explain this phenomenon. The most significant is that few returnees anticipate reverse culture shock. When we expect a stressful event, we cope with it much better. We rehearse our reactions, think through the course of adjustment, and consider alternative ways to deal with the stressful event. We are prepared both physically and emotionally for the worst that could happen.

Most sojourners are already expecting stress before they leave home. They know they will miss family and friends, and they are anxious about adjusting to new food, a different language, unfamiliar public transportation, and so forth. On the other hand, few sojourners worry about returning home.

Those who adjust best overseas and are the most successful have probably changed the most during their sojourn. They have more confidence in their abilities to adapt and succeed and thus are the least likely to be anxious about returning home. For example, adolescent children usually adjust very quickly and easily to a new culture, yet they tend to experience much greater reentry stress than their parents.

In an overseas culture, host nationals expect newcomers to make mistakes and be different. Most intuitively understand that the sojourner will experience stress adapting to the new physical and social environment and will long for friends and family back home.

At home, everyone expects the returnee to fit in quickly. They are much less tolerant of mistakes and have little empathy for the difficulties of reverse culture shock—such problems are not expected or accepted. The honeymoon period may last only a few days or hours.

The Causes of Reverse Culture Shock

1. The breakdown of interpersonal communication

The causes of reverse culture shock are quite similar to those of culture shock.

A breakdown of interpersonal communication again occurs, resulting in enormous frustration and pain. Most returnees do not realize that this breakdown is the cause of their distress. Consequently, they are unaware of what provokes the reactions commonly labeled as symptoms of reverse culture shock.

When people communicate, they send messages, not meanings. The meanings are in their heads, and the messages merely try to express them. If two people experience the world in a similar way, their messages will take similar or parallel forms. If they experience the world differently, their messages usually take different forms. What would be a message to one person may have no meaning whatsoever to another. Even which messages are noticed may be different in different cultures. Of course, most people assume that everyone else pays attention to the same messages as they do and that everyone gives the messages the same meaning.

Americans are primarily verbally oriented people. When they communicate face-to-face, they pay attention to what is said and tend to be less consciously aware of nonverbal messages — tone of voice, posture, gestures, facial expressions, social distance, touch, eye contact, and so forth. On the other hand, non-Western people often pay much greater attention to nonverbal messages and consciously send them more frequently in interpersonal communication.

If an African spends a great deal of time in the United States, he becomes much more conscious of verbal messages and decreases his awareness of nonverbal messages. In the United States, his verbal abilities are highly rewarded and reinforced while his nonverbal subtlety only leads to confusion. Conversely, an American having spent time in Africa returns home adept at sending and receiving nonverbal messages yet perhaps less conscious of direct verbal messages.

While in the United States, the African sojourner tacitly learns to maintain an arm's length when talking and to offer a brisk handshake, almost immediately released. Upon his return to Africa, he is met by family and friends at the airport. His cousin rushes to shake his hand and continues greeting him without releasing his grip. Others crowd around him as they welcome him home. He tries to pull away from his cousin's grip and backs away from those who are talking to him. The returnee suddenly feels as if everyone is very pushy and intruding on his personal space.

His friends and family suddenly realize how he has changed. He seems cold and standoffish (冷淡的). They consciously notice how he will not hold hands and how he steps back when they try to talk to him. The returnee may be quite oblivious (没有注意到) to the nonverbal messages he is sending or why he feels uncomfortable.

While in the United States, the African student learned that Americans are often very rushed and thus it is perfectly polite to greet others with a quick "hi." At home, people expect him to engage in more personal conversation, asking "How are you?" "How is your family?" "How are you feeling?" Of course, a polite person would respond with a great deal more than "fine." The returnee finds that others perceive him as rude or abrupt because he no longer is comfortable engaging in lengthy greetings. If he "properly" greeted everyone, he would never get to work on time.

In the United States, frankness and honest feedback are appreciated. Americans do not want to guess at one's response to a question and they feel uncomfortable with ambiguous or nonverbal answers. A clearly stated "yes" or "no" is usually very polite to an American while indirection, subtlety, or "maybes" are often experienced as inscrutable or deceptive.

2. The "Uncle Charlie Syndrome"

Cleveland et al. describe a common experience of returnees. In the words of an interviewee:

"In my hometown, there are probably many people who still don't realize the world is round. I remember when we got home from Moscow people asked me how it was there, but before I could open my mouth, they would begin telling me how Uncle Charlie had broken his arm. They profess interest in things abroad, but they really aren't interested."

Sojourners want to share their overseas experiences, yet trying to do so is a painfully difficult task. After a few days of listening to anecdotes, viewing photos, and receiving gifts, most friends and family members lose interest. Very often the most meaningful experiences really cannot be communicated. These messages have little meaning to those who have never actually lived overseas. It is somewhat like trying to describe the wonder of a sunset to someone who is blind.

The parochialism (狭隘) of the home society becomes more obvious than ever before to these sojourners, especially in contrast with the more global perspective acquired while away. Although they have discovered many hidden aspects of their own culture by going overseas and have broadened their view of the world, they have also returned more critical of their own society. To adapt overseas, sojourners had to be more tolerant of other points of views, change many of their attitudes, and open their minds to new ways of perceiving reality. Ironically, this tolerance and open-mindedness is not always extended to those back home.

While Uncle Charlie's broken arm may seem insignificant to the returnee, it was probably a traumatic event for the family. The returnee's lack of interest in Uncle Charlie's broken arm may be very unsettling to those back home.

3. Other communication barriers

Students returning from the United States to poorer countries are sometimes faced with envy and resentment from those who did not have the opportunity to travel abroad. Often, the image of America held by those at home is based upon an assumption that everyone there has great wealth, and it may be anticipated that returnees will carry back expensive gifts for all.

These students may have written glowing letters home describing their experiences. Sometimes they have failed to describe their financial struggles, thereby reinforcing the perception that they have ample funds. Perceived to be carrying home the "golden fleece (金羊毛，喻指财富)," the students may be faced with a host of new obligations — including paying school fees for younger siblings, living in a style typical of a college graduate, and providing loans to older family members. They cannot hope to play these new and unexpected roles or to match the new identity ascribed to them by friends and family.

Students who have remained overseas for a long period face a barrier of time separating them from family and friends. To get on with life, some loved ones left at home may have needed to go through a cycle of grief for the departed sojourner. They have experienced the anger and depression that often characterize grief, and have psychologically "buried" the sojourner. Upon the sojourner's return, it is as if a ghost had appeared. Intimate relationships cannot simply continue from where they were at departure. They must be evaluated and developed again, taking into account the change that has occurred because of the sojourn.

Reactions or "Symptoms"

Most returnees take for granted their ability to effectively communicate with friends and family. The breakdown of communication causes frustration and pain, which, in turn, lead to the physical and psychological reactions associated with stress. Because this stress is not expected, reactions are usually much more severe than those of entry culture shock.

Initially, many returnees may withdraw from others, fantasize about returning overseas, or sleep a great deal. The returnee is often perplexed (困惑的) by these subconscious reactions to the breakdown of communication.

A sense of being out of control is very common. Gregarious (爱交际的) sojourners may find themselves avoiding others at home. Fantasies begin to preoccupy them, and returnees may suspect that they acquired some illness overseas accounting for excessive sleeping. Reactions to the situation begin to control returnees and, being unaware of the cause of these reactions, they may not consider alternative ways to cope with the original breakdown of communication.

Returnees to non-Western cultures often find this period especially difficult because they cannot flee or avoid others. While there is great respect for privacy in the United States, this attitude is rare in cultures that emphasize kinship and friendship ties over the individual. Americans might not find it strange for someone to avoid others for a few days. In many cultures of Africa, Latin America, and Asia, to do so is almost impossible and would be viewed as a bizarre behavior.

They cannot escape others permanently, sleep away their days, or go back overseas again. They remain trapped in a painful situation that appears hopeless. At this point, a second reaction usually develops — a "fight" response or aggression. While perfectly normal under the circumstances, many returnees are confused by their own aggressive behavior. Some even feel guilty, especially returnees to the United States, where anger is often equated with irrationality.

Because of the value placed on rationality and the overwhelming sense of guilt and loss of control caused by such reactions, some returnees internalize or deny their anger. This denial actually makes matters worse — depression is often attributed to internalized anger. Adding to the problem, hopelessness and lack of control cause some returnees to feel helpless. They can perceive no way of coping with their feelings and are unaware of what is causing them to behave in such irrational ways. Their sense of hopelessness, helplessness, and lack of control causes them to simply give up trying to control the situation. They learn to be helpless, and learned helplessness is also often considered a major factor in depression.

Many other reactions occur to the breakdown of communication. For example, returnees may neurotically (神经过敏地) distort and deny the complexity of reentry. Some behave as if they have never been abroad, much like a soldier who refuses to accept the reality of battlefield experiences once at home. Such a person denies the impact of the experience and refuses to even try discussing it with others.

Other sojourners go to the opposite extreme. They never actually return home, or they deny they are at home. The Nigerian returnee who studied in London wears three-piece tweed suits, smokes a pipe, and drinks tea every afternoon and scotch in the evening. He speaks in an exaggerated British accent and drones (单调乏味地讲述) on constantly about how wonderful everything was in London and how terrible everything is in Lagos. Of course, he forgets the bad times he had while abroad and ignores the many positive aspects of his homeland.

An interesting modification of these distortions and denials is illustrated by a group of young men in The Gambia who are referred to as the "Been-Tos." They gather nightly in a small bar and unconsciously exclude those who have never sojourned overseas. Conversation is almost entirely about where they have been to — some have been to London, others to New York, and so forth. They constantly relive their overseas adventures, much like many Peace Corps volunteers who have formed their own "Been-To" cliques (小集团) in the United States.

(Adapted from "Culture, Communication and Conflict: Readings in Intercultural Relations" by Gary Weaver)

Questions

1. Do you believe that reverse culture shock is worse than culture shock? Why or why not?

2. What is "Uncle Charlie Syndrome?" Do you have this experience going back home from university?

3. What are the major reentry symptoms?

Intercultural Communication Competence

It is a luxury to be understood.

— *R.W. Emerson*

We should not judge another person until we have walked two moons in his moccasins.

— *Native American proverb*

Intercultural communication involves my indicating to you the rules which govern my understanding and behavior of my culture, and you indicating to me the rules which govern them in your culture, and our showing a mutual respect of their similarities and differences.

— *S. S. King*

PART ❶ Warm Up

1. Watch a video clip to get some ideas about the concept of intercultural communication competence as well as its components.
2. Read the following statements carefully and ask yourself if you have familiar perceptions. Discuss with your group members what effects such statements may have upon intercultural communication.

1. All Americans eat nothing but McDonald's and KFC.
2. Japanese men are all short and workaholics.
3. The French are romantic and drink wine constantly.
4. Italians are affectionate and eat nothing but pizza and spaghetti.
5. Germans are rigorous, strictly-disciplined, and arrogant.
6. Russians spend their days and nights guzzling vodka.
7. All Jews are wealthy, unscrupulous, and smart at business.
8. Every Chinese person knows martial arts.

PART ❷ Readings

Passage 1 ▶ Intercultural Communication Competence

Although the study of intercultural communication can be dated back to the works of political scientists and anthropologists in the 1940s and 1950s, the topic of intercultural communication competence remains a fresh area. Intercultural communication competence is the only means whereby we can move beyond cultural differences in order to succeed in intercultural interactions. But, "What is intercultural communication competence?" Before we answer this question we first need to understand what is "competence."

Definition of Competence

One early study in 1959 considers competence "an organism's capacity to interact effectively with its environment." Competence was viewed as a basic human need and the measure of competence was proposed to be the degree to which a person produces the intended effect from interaction with the environment.

Competence was also defined as the acquired ability to interact effectively. This definition sees communication competence as an inherent ability that relates neither to personal intellect nor to education. However, in 1969, it was proposed that communication competence increases through socialization and that we learn it incidentally[1], rather than through deliberate effort.

Later, the concept of competence was further expanded to include both interactants by defining competence as "the ability to relate effectively to self and others." That is, to be competent, we must not only feel we are competent, but our ability should be observed and confirmed by our counterparts.

In 1977, Wiemann, a famous scholar, conceptualized[2] communicative competence as "the ability of an interactant to choose among available communicative behaviors in order that he may successfully accomplish his own goals." All these conceptualizations focus on perceived effectiveness in an interaction.

Whereas some scholars conceive of communication competence as a function of perceived effectiveness, others look at communication competence from the viewpoint of appropriateness. For example, Backlund, another scholar from the U.S., reviewed the various definitions of communication competence and defined communication competence as "the ability to demonstrate the knowledge of the socially appropriate communicative behavior in a given situation."

In 1978, one set of rules for appropriateness was offered by researchers:

- Say just enough — not too little or too much.
- Don't say something that's false — or speak about something for which you lack evidence.
- Relate your contribution to the topic and situation.
- Be clear about what you are saying, and say it "with dispatch[3]."

Notes
[1] （伴随某事）偶然发生地
[2] 使概念化
[3] 迅速而有效地

These rules stressed the four elements of appropriateness: quality, quantity, relevancy, and manner of message sending in interaction. Thus, communication competence is comprised of two elements: effectiveness and appropriateness.

Definition of Intercultural Communication Competence

In addition to looking at communication competence as effective and appropriate interaction, intercultural communication scholars place more emphasis on contextual factors. They conceived of communication competence not only as effective and appropriate interaction between people, but as effective and appropriate interaction between people who belong to particular environments. This orientation resembles that of communication scholars who emphasize competence as a context-specific behavior. Thus, we conceive of intercultural communication competence as "the ability to effectively and appropriately execute communication behaviors to elicit a desired response in a specific environment." This definition shows that competent persons must not only know how to interact effectively and appropriately with people and environment, but also know how to fulfill their own communication goals using this ability.

The Components of Intercultural Competence

The summary of previous research suggests that competent intercultural communication is contextual; it produces behaviors that are both appropriate and effective; and it requires sufficient knowledge, suitable motivations, and skilled actions. Let's examine each of these components.

Context: Intercultural competence is contextual. An impression or judgment that a person is interculturally competent is made with respect to both a specific relational context and a particular situational context. Competence is not independent of the relationships and situations within which communication occurs. Thus, competence is not an individual attribute[④]; rather, it is a characteristic of the association between individuals. It is possible, therefore, for someone to be perceived as highly competent in one set of intercultural interactions and only moderately competent in another. For example, a Canadian woman living with a family in India might establish

Notes
④ 特质

competent relationships with female family members but be unable to relate well to the male members.

Appropriateness and Effectiveness: Both interpersonal competence and intercultural competence require behaviors that are appropriate and effective. By appropriate we mean those behaviors that are regarded as proper and suitable given the expectations generated by a given culture, the constraints of the specific situation, and the nature of the relationship between the interactants. By effective we mean those behaviors that lead to the achievement of desired outcomes.

Knowledge, Motivations, and Actions: Intercultural competence requires sufficient knowledge, suitable motivations, and skilled actions. Each of these components alone is insufficient to achieve intercultural competence.

Knowledge refers to the cognitive information you need to have about the people, the context, and the norms of appropriateness that operate in a specific culture. Without such knowledge, it is unlikely that you will interpret correctly the meanings of other people's messages, nor will you be able to select behaviors that are appropriate and that allow you to achieve your objectives. Consequently, you will not be able to determine what the appropriate and effective behaviors are in a particular context. The kinds of knowledge that are important include culture-general and culture-specific information. The former provides insights into the intercultural communication process abstractly and can therefore be a very powerful tool in making sense of cultural practices, regardless of the cultures involved. Culture-specific information is used to understand a particular culture. Such knowledge should include information about the forces that maintain the culture's uniqueness and facts about the cultural patterns that predominate.

Motivations include the overall set of emotional associations that people have as they anticipate and actually communicate interculturally. As with knowledge, different aspects of the emotional terrain contribute to the achievement of intercultural competence. Human emotional reactions include both feelings and intentions. Feelings of happiness, sadness, eagerness, anger, tension, surprise, confusion, relaxation, and joy are among the many emotions that can accompany the intercultural communication experience. Feelings involve your general sensitivity to other cultures and your attitudes toward the specific culture and individual with whom you must interact. Intensions are what guide your choices in a particular intercultural interaction. Your intensions are the goals, plans, objectives, and desires that focus and direct your behavior. Intensions are often affected by the stereotypes[5] you have of people from other cultures because stereotypes reduce the number of choices and interpretations you are willing to consider.

Actions refer to the actual performance of those behaviors that are regarded as appropriate and effective. Thus, you can have the necessary information, be motivated by the appropriate feelings and intentions, and still lack the behavioral skills necessary to achieve competence. For example, students from other cultures who enroll in basic public speaking classes often have an excellent understanding of the theory of speech construction. In addition, they have a positive attitude toward learning U.S. speaking skills; they want to do well and are willing to work hard in preparation. Unfortunately, their speaking skills sometimes make it difficult for them to execute the delivery of a speech with the level of skill and precision that they would like.

(Adapted from "Foundations of Intercultural Communication" by Guo-Ming Chen & W. J. Statost, and from "Intercultural Competence: Interpersonal Communication Across Cultures" by M. W. Lustig & J. Koester)

Notes
⑤ 成见

Questions

1. What are the elements of competence?
2. What is intercultural communication competence? In what way is it different from competence?
3. Why is intercultural communication competence contextual?
4. What does appropriateness and effectiveness mean in intercultural communication competence?

Passage 2 ▶ Potential Barriers to Effective Intercultural Communication

Interacting with people from diverse cultures is often difficult and more often than not frustrating, and misunderstanding seems unavoidable. Why is intercultural communication so difficult? This is because there are potential problems and barriers that lie in the process of intercultural communication. Identification of these problems will help us to avoid or to reduce breakdowns in intercultural communication.

The Assumption of Similarity

The assumption of similarity is one of the biggest barriers to successful intercultural communication. The assumption that we are all alike instead of being different seriously hinders effective communication across cultures and as Barna, a famous scholar, once pointed out, "the notion 'People are people' is as dangerous as it is sentimental [①]." As a matter of fact, each member of a society is culture-bound and culture-specific. As we naively assume that people of other cultures are like us, we tend to automatically use the norms or rules underlying our thinking, behaving and feeling as standard to judge, evaluate and interpret the behavior or message, both verbal and nonverbal, of people from different cultures, and in doing so, misunderstanding is inevitable.

To illustrate this, let's examine how individuals of different cultures interpret a smile. To a Chinese male in the U.S., a smile is likely to indicate interest or affection. If a girl smiles at a male stranger in China, it is likely to be taken as expressing interest. However, a smile from a male on the street at a female stranger could possibly be seen as rude or even lewd. For Japanese students newly arrived in the U.S., it would be rude to smile at people they are unfamiliar with. A smile from an American student would likewise make Arabian students embarrassed because they feel they may have dressed inappropriately. How will American students react to such a response to their friendly smile then? An American student remarked "In general it seems to me that foreign people are not necessarily snobs but are very unfriendly. Some class members have told me that I shouldn't smile at others while passing by them on the street. To me I can't stop smiling. It's just natural to be smiling and friendly. I can see now why people tend to stick to their own. Foreigners

Notes
① 情感的，情绪的
（非理智的）

are impossible to know. It's like the Americans are big bad wolves. How do Americans break this barrier? We want to have friends from all over the world but how do we start becoming friends without offending them or scaring them off like sheep?"

Stereotype

Stereotypes are the second barrier to effective intercultural communication. In stereotyping others, it is believed that all the people of a given group share the same characteristics. Stereotypes may help reduce the threat of the unknown by making the unknown world predictable as they provide conceptual bases from which to make sense of the stranger and the stimuli or the situation or context in which one is located. However stereotypes can be stumbling block[2] for communication as they simplify the perception of people from diverse cultures. The application of stereotypes to all or most members of a particular group in intercultural communication may result in a tendency to ignore differences among the individual members of the group. Stereotypes can also lead to mistakes in interpretations and expectations about the behaviors of people from different cultures. For example, if we perceive all Chinese people as polite, Italians as emotional, Russians as alcoholic, Americans as generous, British as cold and standoffish[3], New Zealanders as casual and laid-back, or blacks as athletic, women as indirect in communication, sportsmen as dimwits[4], blondes as empty-headed, Japanese women as ideal homemakers, and gays as a danger to children, we are stereotyping, which may likely lead us to ignoring the specific characteristics of an individual. These stereotypes are called negative stereotypes that interfere with an objective view of the stimuli of others.

The Tendency to Evaluate and Judge or to Approve or Disapprove

The tendency to evaluate and judge or to approve or disapprove forms the third potential barrier in the process of intercultural communication. This tendency in fact grows out what is called ethnocentrism, which is characterized by the belief that one's own group or culture is superior to all other groups or cultures or one's own culture seems to be right and proper ("my way is proper and right"). To different extent, we all have the tendency of

Notes
② 障碍物
③ 冷漠的
④ 傻子

consciously or unconsciously interpreting, evaluating, judging, approving or disapproving others' behavior by the standards or norms of our own culture. This natural bias hinders an open-minded attention to look at the attitudes and behavior patterns from the other's worldview. The communication cutoff caused by immediate evaluation is heightened when feeling and emotions are deeply involved; yet this is just the time when listening with understanding is most needed. It is important to take a non-evaluative and non-judgmental attitude in the process of communication.

Automatic Transfer

Automatic transfer of the norms and rules from one's own culture to the use of the target language constitutes the fourth potential barrier. We are born and bred up in our own culture and the rules and norms of speaking and writing have become our unconscious behavior. Then, when thrown into a strange culture, the Chinese unconsciously adopt Chinese cultural rules and norms in communication in the American or British context, for example. We may greet American acquaintances with, "Have you eaten?" or "Where are you going?" and address American friends by their last names. Likewise, the Chinese tend to transfer to a different cultural context the Chinese ways of apologizing, requesting, approving, disapproving, agreeing, disagreeing, saying thanks, telephoning, inviting people, and saying goodbye. This transfer also finds its expressions in communication in terms of phonology, semantics, and syntactic rules. And transfer is also popular in writing, particularly the organization of discourse patterns. This automatic and unconscious transfer more often than not results in misinterpretation, and offence to people from a different culture.

High Uncertainty and Anxiety

High uncertainty and anxiety is the fifth deterrent[5] to effective intercultural communication. Uncertainty refers to cognitive response to the stimuli from a strange situation or environment while anxiety refers to response to the stimuli from strange situations or environments. Uncertainty occurs because we are unable to predict the behaviors of others while anxiety, the feeling of being uneasy, tense, nervous, worried or even apprehensive,

Notes
⑤ 遏止因素

may result from being afraid of failure in communication. High uncertainty and anxiety can be translated into substantial discomfort with others. Yoka, a Japanese student who was studying in the States expressed her feelings about her uncertainty and anxiety in her intercultural communication as follows:

> I came home from class every day and cried my first month at the university. No one seemed to be able to understand me and I couldn't understand the professor or any of the students. When I first met my roommate, she hugged me. I felt very strange. I never hug anyone, not even my parents when I left for America. Most of the American students wanted to go and get drunk on weekend. I got so sick of everyone smiling at me for no reason. I felt very dumb. Even though I studied English at school in Tokyo, no one could tell. Everyone spoke so fast and always wanted to know if I liked it better here than in Japan. I was exhausted after each day and would fall asleep rather than read my books or go out and socialize.

Though we are never free from uncertainty and anxiety, a moderate level of uncertainty and anxiety is desirable so that we may take steps to improve our communication and adaptation to another culture.

Misinterpretation of Nonverbal Behavior

The misinterpretation of nonverbal behavior is the sixth barrier to effective intercultural communication. As we have mentioned before, nonverbal messages are also important in the mutual understanding in intercultural communication. Most nonverbal behavior is acquired throughout the socialization process and is therefore culture specific. Hence, in intercultural communication, we may find ourselves to be at odds with people from different cultures, in areas ranging from understanding of eye contact and touch to body posture and emotional expressions and interpersonal distance. We tend to misinterpret the message in the form of nonverbal behavior because we are limited by a lack of knowledge of nonverbal behavior of the different culture and because these behaviors are often ambiguous, spontaneous and often beyond unconscious awareness and control.

The awareness that these barriers hinder effective intercultural communication helps us avoid them. However, stanching[⑥] their influence is difficult and some of them are almost unavoidable. We have to have strategies to overcome these barriers, such as the development of sensitivity toward diversity, the building up of supportive communication behaviors, the training of skills to avoid the trap of stereotyping, the cultivation of open-mindedness, the use of descriptive approach toward stimuli in a new environment, and the development of tolerance for ambiguity and of intercultural competence, only then can effective communication be addressed.

(Adapted from "Gateway to Intercultural Communication" by Song Li)

Notes
⑥ 止住（尤指血）的流出

Questions

1. Which potential problem do you think is most likely to lead to misunderstanding in intercultural communication?

2. What does the word "transfer" mean in the context?

3. Have you experienced high anxiety and uncertainty when encountering a person from a different culture? How did you deal with your feelings of anxiety and uncertainty?

4. Can you give more examples that cause misunderstanding in intercultural communication in nonverbal behavior?

5. Can you think of any other potential problems that will hinder intercultural communication?

Passage 3 ▶ Improving Intercultural Communication

So far we have already discussed many cases of intercultural communication in which problems arise because people involved are culturally different. All this suggests that intercultural communication is difficult. Now you may ask what we can do about it if intercultural communication is inevitable in our times. In the following, suggestions from scholars working in this field are offered to improve intercultural communication.

Know Yourself

As simplistic as it sounds, what you bring to the communication event greatly influences the success or failure of that event. Although the idea of knowing yourself is common, it is nevertheless crucial to improving intercultural communication. The novelist James Baldwin said it best when he wrote, "The questions which one asks oneself begin, at last, to illuminate the world, and become one's key to the experience of others.

Your first step toward introspection[①] should begin with your own culture, regardless of what that culture might be. Remember, we are products of our culture — and that culture helps control communication. An awareness of our culture along with examples of contrasting cultures contributes greatly to our understanding of ourselves as cultural beings.

You should identify those attitudes, prejudices, and opinions that we all carry around and that bias the way the world appears to us. Knowing our likes, dislikes, and the degrees of personal ethnocentrism enables us to place them out in the open so that we can detect the ways in which these attitudes influence communication. Hidden personal premises[②], be they directed at ideas, people, or entire cultures, are often the cause of many of our difficulties in understanding others.

The third step in "knowing yourself" is learning to recognize your communication style — the manner in which you present yourself to others. It is somewhat more difficult than simply identifying your prejudices and predispositions[③]. It involves discovering the kind of image we portray to the rest of the world. Ask yourself "How do I communicate and how do others perceive me?" If you perceive you in another way, serious problems can arise. If, for instance, you see yourself as patient and calm, but you appear rushed and anxious, you will have a hard time understanding why people respond to you as they do. Our most taken-for-granted behaviors often are hidden from consciousness.

Seek to Understand Different Languages

Since language is so important to successful communication, whenever possible, both parties involved in intercultural communication should seek a common language and attempt to understand cultural differences in using the

Notes
① 内省
② 假设
③ 倾向

language. If you plan to spend some time around people from other cultures, try to learn their language. You would be far more effective if you could speak Spanish when doing business in Mexico. Moreover, you should keep in mind that there is more to language than vocabulary, syntax, and dialects. Language is more than a vehicle of communication; it teaches one a culture's lifestyle, ways of thinking, and different patterns of interacting. In addition, you should also realize there are different styles of "talk." One is not right and the others wrong — they are only different.

Develop Empathy

The next suggestion for improvement is to develop empathy[④] — be able to see things from the point of view of others so that we can better know and adjust to the other people.

Perhaps the most common of all barriers to empathy is a constant self-focus. It is difficult to gather information about the other person, and to reflect on that information, if we are consumed with thoughts of ourselves. Attending to our own thoughts, as if they were the only ones that mattered, uses much of the energy that we should direct toward our communication partner.

Many of the hindrance to empathy can be traced back to a lack of motivation. This problem might well be the most difficult to conquer. We are most motivated to respond to people who are close to us both physically and emotionally. We are primarily concerned about our families. As our personal circle widens, it includes relatives and friends. Interest in other people then moves to neighbors and other members of the community. As we get further and further away from people in our immediate circle, we tend to find it hard to empathize. Think for a moment about your reaction to the news that someone you know had been seriously injured in an automobile accident versus your response to reading that 700,000 people were suffering from severe famine in the Sudan. In most instances you would be more motivated to learn about your friend than about the people thousands of miles away in Africa. Although this is a normal reaction, it often keeps us from trying to understand the experiences of people far removed from our personal sphere.

For intercultural communication to be successful, we must all learn to go beyond personal boundaries and try to learn about the experiences of

Notes

④ 感情移入，同感（对他人的感情、经历等的想像力和感受力）

people who are not part of our daily lives. We must realize that we live in an interconnected world, and we must therefore be motivated to understand everyone — regardless of how much we seem separated from them by either distance or culture.

To be successful as an intercultural communicator, you must develop empathy, and that can be cultivated only if you become sensitive to the values and customs of the culture with which you are interacting. Again we remind you that empathy can be increased if you resist the tendency to interpret the other's verbal and nonverbal actions from you culture's orientation. Learn to suspend, or at least keep in check, the cultural perspective that is unique to your experiences. Knowing how the frame of reference of other cultures differs from your own will assist you in accurately reading what meaning lies behind words and actions. The action or words of others may appear unusual (or even downright ridiculous). However, you can avoid conflict by understanding and respecting their viewpoint. This does not mean that you have to agree with them. When you can see their perspective, you are better able to understand the situation. So you are better equipped to provide a mutually agreeable solution to the problem.

(Adapted from "Intercultural Communication in English" by Xu Lisheng)

Questions

1. Why knowing yourself is crucial to improving intercultural communication?
2. Do you think learning a foreign language is sufficient for intercultural understanding? Why or why not?
3. What is empathy? How can you develop empathy?
4. Can you offer more suggestions on improving intercultural communication?

PART ❸ Exercises

Section **A** ▶ Culture Quiz

Watch the video clip about intercultural communication competence and fill in the blanks with the words or phrases you see.

Intercultural Competence is the ability to _____ in intercultural situations; it is supported by _____.		
A _____ Set	A _____ Set	A _____ Set
The ability to _____.	The ability to _____.	The ability to _____.
Components of the Dimension: _____ _____	Components of the Dimension: _____ _____ _____ _____ _____ _____	Components of the Dimension: _____ _____ _____ _____
Example: _____	Example: _____	Example: _____

Section **B** ▶ Group Discussion

Watch the two episodes in the movie of *Gua Sha Treatment* and discuss the components of intercultural communication competence by filling in the following table.

ICC in *Gua Sha Treatment*		
	Episode 1	Episode 2
Context		
Appropriateness		
Effectiveness		
Knowledge		
Motivation		
Action		

Section C▶ Intercultural Practice

You will be presented with a situation and four possible utterances underneath. Read the description of each situation with the utterances and decide which utterance is the most appropriate one for that situation.

1. You have spent an afternoon with your foreign teacher, Mr. Good. As you go, Mr. Good says, "Do drop around and visit us some time." You reply,

    A. "Yes, of course, if I am free."

    B. "Thank you. I will come at 7 p.m. on Monday."

    C. "I will come anytime, if you like."

    D. "Thank you, I will."

2. Suppose you are at the home of your English teacher, Mr. Savior. Mr. Savior says, "We are so glad to have you with us today." You reply,

    A. "Thank you."

    B. "I'm glad to be here."

    C. "I want to see you long ago."

    D. "I've bothered you too much."

3. Xiao Ma is an interpreter. One day a foreign visitor, Mr. Brown, talks to him. Mr. Brown says, "Your English is quite fluent." Ma should reply,

    A. "Thank you. It's kind of you to say so."

B. "No not at all."

C. "No, no, my English is poor."

D. "Oh, no. Far from that, I still have a long way to go."

4. Which topic is more appropriate to discuss immediately after an introduction?

A. Politics.

B. Religion.

C. Marital status.

D. Occupation.

5. When introduced to a senior professor or to the parents of a friend, what would you say?

A. "Hi! Glad to know you."

B. "Hello" and bow.

C. "Hello, it's nice to meet you," and then shake hands.

D. "How are you?"

6. You've just been asked out to dinner but you don't want to go with the person who invited you. You might say'

A. "I don't think so. I already have plans."

B. "No, I really don't enjoy being with you."

C. "I'm dieting so I mustn't go out to eat."

D. "Thanks a lot but I'm busy tonight."

7. A and B are neighbors. A says, "My cat knocked over my new vase this morning." B replies,

A. "What a shame!"

B. "A shame."

C. "Shame on you."

D. "Shame!"

8. Your friend's mother, Mrs. Keeler, asked if you would like something to eat. What would you say to refuse politely?

A. "No, thank you. You are so kind."

B. "Oh, no. Mrs. Keeler."

C. "No, thanks, I've just had lunch."

D. "I'm full now and have no room for any more."

(Adapted from "Intercultural Communication" by Zhang Ailing)

Section D▸ Case Studies

Case 1

Rosamine and Merita are from two different cultures. They are talking about one aspect of their family life and seem to have different points of view.

Rosamine: I think it's terrible that in your country children leave parents when they are so young. Something that shocks me even more is that many parents want their children to leave home. I can't understand why children and parents don't like each other in your country?

Merita: In your country parents don't allow their children to become independent. Parents keep their children protected until the children get married. How are young people in your country supposed to learn about life that way?

(Adapted from "Intercultural Communication" by Zhang Ailing)

Questions

1. Who do you agree with, Rosamine or Merita? Why?
2. Some young people in China still prefer to live with their parents even after getting married. What do you think of this phenomenon?

Case 2

Watch the video clip about cultural conflicts and answer the following questions.

Questions

1. What are the cultural conflicts that have been shown in the video?
2. What are the causes of the conflicts?
3. What kind of suggestions would you like to give to the people involved in the conflicts in the video?

PART ❹   Additional Reading

Cultural Literacy: Understanding and Respect for the Cultural Aspects of Sustainability

Cultural literacy includes cultural competence but adds to it the ability to critically reflect on, and if necessary bring about change in, one's own culture. It also includes the ability to critically analyse the behaviours of dominant cultures in relation to other cultures, for instance, the impact of globalization or cross-cultural partnerships on local cultures around the world. There are four key cultural literacy skills:

Cross-Cultural Awareness

Within the enormous cultural diversity that exists on Earth there are cultures which manage to fulfil human needs from the local environment in ways which are sustainable, or at least, more sustainable than the consumerism-based cultures. Cultural literacy therefore includes the ability to critically examine other cultures and gain ideas about sustainability from them. Learning about another culture can be as simple as using the internet or consulting academic literature or popular media. However, this knowledge is a superficial understanding of another culture, not unlike the tourist gaze phenomenon where learning can be viewed as inauthentic and artificial.

Rather than learning about other cultures, a deeper and more respectful learning for sustainability can be gained by "paralleling" different cultural traditions, beliefs and social systems with the consumerist cultures of the West, and then utilising this learning as a tool for critical reflection on aspects of both Western culture and the paralleled cultures. The word "parallel" is used to provide a more egalitarian view of cultural examination than the value-laden "comparison" which insinuates one may be more appropriate, successful, valuable than the other.

Time spent understanding and "paralleling" different cultural traditions can be extremely valuable when carrying out international sustainable development projects, both to avoid damage to the local culture and to draw on aspects of the culture which are already sustainable. One example of such a project is the co-operation between Ugandan local communities; Welsh Water and WaterAid. In this partnership, the Ugandan communities continued their cultural outdoor lifestyles but worked with the outside agencies to enhance sustainable living practices and increase the quality of life for communities in relation to health, education, environmental protection and conservation. Sustainable technologies from both Western and Ugandan cultures were combined with the sustainable local traditional lifestyles and environmental practices of the Ugandan culture to implement sustainable development. This project can be utilised as an example of a beneficial use of cultural literacy for sustainability as it does not use sustainable development for the sole purpose of increasing trade and growth for Western countries, but rather uses it to maintain local cultural and social sustainability.

Not all projects which come under the label of 'sustainable development' are beneficial to all cultures involved, it is important for learners to view partnerships for sustainability between the West and developing countries as intervention (which could potentially be negative) rather than development (which has intrinsically positive connotations in the West). One exercise that can help raise awareness of how sustainable development can be tainted by Western economic values of market expansion is to involve students in critical analysis of how sustainable development is represented by transnational corporations. For instance, a recent Kenco Coffee advertisement claims that the company assists local communities in sustainable development through their trade with them. This image of sustainable development is predominantly Western with Western style houses popping up out of rainforests, Western style classrooms (desks and blackboards) in the middle of a culture with exceptionally good natural environment for learning outside the classroom, and water gushing out of a Western style irrigation system indicating that it is now possible to waste a valuable resource now that it is "on tap." The underlying message is that "valuable," "better" or "progressive" development involves becoming more like the (unsustainable) societies of the west. Cultural literacy can help prepare learners to contribute to developing sustainable societies that reflect and sustain local cultures rather than imposing dominant cultural values and social systems from the West.

Local Cultural Awareness

Cultural awareness and respect is not just a cross-cultural skill. The ability to accept and respect knowledge within local cultures and communities is also necessary for developing cultural literacy. There may be knowledge and skills for living sustainably that are already embedded in the traditions of local cultures and passed on intergenerationally through non-formal education. Formal education tends to place little value on such practical knowledge and skills, preferring instead abstract, technical or generalisable skills suitable for further advancing industrialisation and economic expansion. Education for an ecologically sustainable future requires a shift toward valuing and revitalising local knowledge of how to build self-reliant communities, and protecting this knowledge from the forces of commercialisation and consumerism.

Outdoor learning is particularly suitable for drawing on the grassroots expertise in sustainability found in local communities. For instance, a series of outdoor learning short courses developed at the University of Glamorgan focus on sustainability and global citizenship and recognise the extensive and long-term sustainable education already being undertaken in local communities in non-formal and informal learning contexts (Polistina, 2003).

Examples of how formal education can incorporate local grassroots educators include local elders describing the traditional agricultural practices of the region, local mothers working directly with learners for health and sustainability in an outdoor walking group or organic garden; land owners explaining the installation of micro-hydro schemes, and representatives from sustainable communities demonstrating renewable energy and waste systems utilised on their property. Learners can also be inspired to make a shift from fast food, which is both unhealthy and unsustainable, to more sustainable foods such as local, seasonal, organic fruits and vegetables though learning traditional cooking skills in local courses, volunteering in organic edible gardens, working in allotments, and participating in community led health needs assessments.

Critical Reflection and Thinking

Contrary to a culture of specificity and difference is one of hyperculture and indifference. This hyperculture is detrimental to sustainability literacy as it silences the need for self-critique, self-reflection, or reflection on the trajectory that society is taking. Critical reflective thinking is a dialogue between learners and educators on aspects of cultural or social discourse; it considers the experiences of the group as a whole and provides a way of accounting for ourselves. It demonstrates an awareness that actions and events are located in, and explicable by, reference to multiple perspectives as well as influenced by multiple historical and socio-political contexts.

One possible exercise to encourage critical reflective thinking consists of providing learners with a piece of discourse about sustainability from popular media, for example magazines, websites, advertisements or newspapers. Learners write whether they agree, disagree, like, dislike, understand or are confused by the information being provided. Once learners have written down their comments, they take them home without discussing them. At home they are instructed to forget what they have written and reflect on the information from another person's perspective, e.g., a Buddhist, single mother, managing director of a multi-national company, a teenager, and a father in a community in Tanzania. By the time they come back to the group there will be several different perspectives on the same piece of information. In 2007, Seed and his colleagues took this exercise one stage further in the "Council of All Beings," an imaginative exercise where participants wear masks and take on the perspectives of both human and non-human beings affected by environmental issues, including animals, plants, or even whole ecosystems such as rivers. This process can be utilised for any level of education. In higher education the critical reflection and thinking process would naturally progress through levels until a comprehensive and critical examination of information is undertaken with innovative and achievable actions for cultural and social change being provided by the learner.

Personal Skills for Coping with Being a Change Agent

Whilst a cultural shift toward sustainability is being sought globally, in Western society we do not live in a culture that supports the types of widespread changes, diversity of cultural systems or challenges to the status quo that are required for this shift to occur. Learners need to "survive" being change agents for this cultural shift as they will encounter a variety of mental, physical, psychological and emotional battles with those seeking to sustain the status quo. Cultural and social power-brokers may safeguard the prominence of their power positions by discrediting; ridiculing and devaluing groups they perceive to be a threat. Learners and educators therefore need to be empowered to cope with these unreceptive behaviours.

Knowledge itself is a form of power, and learners will need skills in seeking out reliable, up-to-date and accessible information, from the latest climate science to an understanding of neoliberal critiques of sustainability and global citizenship. This requires practical research skills gained through self-directed learning, and can be achieved through mentored projects that learners chose for themselves. Ultimately, the educator becomes a facilitator and enabler of change rather than a disseminator of knowledge.

Having gained knowledge for themselves and reflected deeply on their values within the context of the realities of the 21st century, learners need skills in confident, persuasive public speaking to express their vision of a better world and back it up with evidence. They will also need skills in resisting bullying and harassment, which is, unfortunately, a common response to suggestions that change might be needed. This requires a deep sensitivity to the cultural context and so is an important part of cultural literacy.

Learners' self-confidence and self-esteem can be built through involvement in supportive networks of people working toward common goals, both within local communities and globally in the wider sustainability and global citizenship movement. Being part of a group with shared values can provide learners with valuable social support for their work as cultural change agents and a healthy release for the stresses that they will experience.

(Adapted from "Cultural Literacy: Understanding and Respect for the Cultural Aspects of Sustainability" by K. Polistina)

Questions

1. What is cultural literacy and intercultural literacy?
2. Do you think intercultural literacy is important in the contemporary society? Why or why not?

Intercultural Communication for Education

By nature all men are alike, but by education widely different.

— Chinese saying

Communication is a skill that you can learn. It's like riding a bicycle or typing. If you're willing to work at it, you can rapidly improve the quality of every part of your life.

— Brian Tracy

PART ❶ Warm Up

The following are quotes by some Asian students. Do you agree with their opinions? How much do you know about Western students' learning styles?

I loved my history courses, and really wanted to major in history, but there's no way I could. Everyone in my family wants me to study engineering. It would be very hard for me to go back to India if I didn't major in engineering.

— Indian undergraduate student

Most Singaporeans are here on government scholarships. Even if the sponsoring organization has no minimum GPA requirement for the student, most of us place great emphasis (perhaps too much) on academics — not only in terms of GPA but also graduating with double majors. There's lots of peer pressure in this respect.

— Singaporean undergraduate student

We often avoid classes outside our academic majors, which are mostly in technical fields. In fact, we frequently complain about all those humanities requirements that we have to fulfill.

— Thai undergraduate student

In my country, students learn one way: from teacher to student. In the U.S., students learn many ways. And teachers encourage students to learn with discussions, asking questions whenever you have them, and so on.

— Korean undergraduate student

Sometimes students from China or other Asian countries look quiet in class. But this does not mean they lose concentration. On the contrary, keeping quiet is a way to show respect to the lecturer and is highly valued in China, usually.

— Chinese undergraduate student

(Adapted from "Recognizing and Addressing Cultural Variations in the Classroom," produced by Eberly Center for Teaching Excellence & Educational Innovation of Carnegie Mellon University)

PART ❷ Readings

Passage ❶ Intercultural Communication in Higher Education Context: Pedagogical and Personal Imperatives

The changing global environment has influenced the increasing cultural diversity in many contexts. Like multicultural business institutions, universities have become examples of authentic intercultural contexts. Through the process of internationalization and diversity efforts, universities have been hosting culturally and linguistically diverse groups of students. For their own institutional and pedagogical orientations, campuses ought to consciously address the growing need for healthy and democratic interaction among students, staff and leadership. Institutional effectiveness is hardly possible without dealing with the needs of the workforce. Among the few, healthy intercultural communication, democratic work environment and cultural sensitivity are the most commonly cited needs in the ever growing intercultural world. University campuses are no different in the attempt to create intercultural environment for their own survival and effectiveness. In other words, higher educational institutions should consider the growing demand for intercultural dialogue in their endeavors[①] to respond to the needs of the community they host and meet institutional expectations. In line with these points and to be more specific, there are a number of pedagogical and personal imperatives for the intercultural communication in higher educational contexts.

Notes
① 努力
② 有助于；使处于优势

Pedagogical Imperatives

Universities as institutions, educational policies and curricula as guidelines, teachers as agents of change and students as clients must appropriately respond to the ever-increasing diversity in higher education. Multicultural policies and curricula should be revised to embrace the need for intercultural interactions besides attempts to represent diverse cultural values and dimensions. Through direct inclusion of intercultural courses, contents or examples, it is possible to advantage[②] various groups of students to succeed academically and socially. Extra-curricular activities could also play significant roles by encouraging healthy intercultural dialogue among students.

Concerning the significance of teachers and their instructional methodology, teachers can do a miracle as they are cultural mediators and change agents. Many students learn intercultural qualities such as compassion, empathy, tolerance and democratic ideas and commitment to take part in social and school activities from influential and powerful teachers. These teachers should acquire a comprehensive understanding of ethnic, cultural, religious and social class diversity projected in their classrooms. Teachers in intercultural classrooms ought to: (1) create a sense of community in the classroom which is inclusive and solve conflicts in productive manner, (2) maintain structure which helps students easily grasp order and purposes of daily activities, (3) involve the outside community to build a strong attachment between students and the host community, and lastly (4) push diversity of students in group work to encourage intercultural communication. Universities ought to promote multicultural classrooms which act like an interactive world that encourage instruction and maintain productive dialogue. Such efforts in turn positively enforce instructional outputs. Teachers can use their creativity to promote intercultural interaction and create sound academic environment. For example, they can make groups from various ethnic and cultural identities when they offer group tasks, and they can also reshuffle[3] sitting arrangements in times they feel the arrangement is homogenous[4].

Teachers, as primary agents of change, must demonstrate excellent intercultural competence, cultural sensitivity and academic competence themselves. However, they should not use the classroom as a forum to promote ethnocentric political views; instead they should display citable qualities. As outlined by Samovar & Porter, teachers should understand the diversity of their classroom; know cultural origin of what they bring to the classroom; maintain open dialogue among students; be emphatic and assess acculturation level of their students with respect to students' involvement in popular and own ethnic cultures. As the primary aim of teachers is to deliver instructions effectively, they should understand students' diversity with respect to ethnic, cultural, religious and academic backgrounds. This would assist teachers to clearly identify academic problems of their respective students and support

Notes
[3] 调整
[4] 由同种族人组成的；由同类组成的

them accordingly. Teachers should be emphatic to and feel the needs of their individual students. If they are able to realize and reflect on their classroom behavior and their own actions, they may be able to effect instructions effectively. Finally, by facilitating intercultural communication and making use of diversity in action, teachers can produce competent citizens who can be successful in multiethnic and multicultural working environment.

Personal Development Imperatives

Acquisition of intercultural competence and experiencing intercultural communication are imperatives for personal benefits of the youth. The young generation lives in increasingly globalized world through immigration and online social networking. Universities are meant to work for holistic⑤ development of their students. There are a number of personal developments graduates can gain if they take intercultural communication courses as part of their professional training in universities. First, intercultural competence is about being successful in life. For example, such competence offers people the ability to grasp full awareness of one's own cultural identity and background. Understanding and reflecting on own cultural identity would help understand others. Through intercultural learning, students can have a better picture of the perspectives of others and exercise democratic ideas into their daily life. Second, as intercultural competence is not culture specific or limited to particular set of cultural framework, people with this ability can make use of it whenever they experience new culture and new people in life. Previous cultural and language learning abilities enforce learning and experiencing forthcoming one, locally or in an international arena. This can encourage students to reduce anxiety and integrate into a new culture.

As life and work are inseparable, intercultural learning makes students enjoy job and deal with conflicts successfully. Today, international and multicultural companies are interested in employing multiethnic and multilingual staff. Students with intercultural abilities and second/foreign language skills can work in more than one cultural or geographic territory. Therefore, intercultural learning increases the employability of university graduates and offers them economic advantages too. On the other hand, as life is journey and relationship is unpredictable, intercultural communication

Notes
⑤ 整体的

assists students to make friends from various cultures and locations. A number of people have enjoyed the merits of interethnic or intercultural relationships and marriage. Interculturally competent students find it easy to find friends, date, build relationship and even end in marriage as they develop the abilities necessary to relativize[6] perceptions and manage conflicts productively. Such abilities are central to deny stereotyping and racism. In addition to life and work, intercultural communication positively contributes to the academic performance of students. Students who are anxious of others and possess higher degree of ethnocentric views could hardly benefit from university education which demands team work and from sharing of educational contents and activities. However, students with excellent level of intercultural competence and good intercultural experience can mix themselves with students from other cultures and collaborate with them for academic tasks of mutual interest.

(Adapted from "An Integrative Approach to Intercultural Communication in Context: Empirical Evidences from Higher Education" by Anteneh Tsegaye Ayalew)

Notes

[6] 把…相对起来考虑

Questions

1. Do you think higher education is important for improving students' intercultural communication competence? Why or why not?
2. What do you think teachers should do to help students enhance their intercultural awareness?
3. What do you think students should do themselves to develop their ability of communicating interculturally?
4. How do you think higher education may influence the world with different cultures increasingly integrated?

Passage 2 Intercultural Pedagogy: The Role of Education in Intercultural Communication

A few years ago, I was exploring the fascinating shops along Liulichang

Street in Beijing when my ears detected the sound of crickets① chirping②. Having previously seen crickets in little bamboo cages for sale on the streets of Xining and Xi'an, I decided that a cricket cage would be a great transportable "artifact" to take back to my social studies classroom. I followed the sound of chirps to a small shop, offering a variety of interesting items for sale: rice cups, kites, jade-carved animals, and one loud cricket in a bamboo cage.

While I was attempting to communicate with the shopkeeper, using ridiculous gesturing, another Chinese gentleman in the shop asked, in perfect English, "Do you want to buy something?" As my interpreter communicated my wish, the shopkeeper's smile changed to sadness. He could not sell the cage because he had no other home for the cricket, his treasured pet, which he had bred and reared.

The photograph I took of the man and his cricket now reminds me not to make assumptions about the cross-cultural meanings of words. Dogs and cats are not always kept as pets in some areas of China. Crickets are pets, to be cherished as people in my culture dote on their dogs and cats.

Miscommunication can breed misunderstanding. For another example, a few years earlier I was in Venice, touring St. Mark's Square. The orchestras③ were filling the air with beautiful music, and the pigeons were dive-bombing the crowds. I tried to enter the cathedral but was refused admittance because my arms were bare. I had purposefully worn a skirt, assuming that was proper dress for the occasion. What I had failed to grasp was that the underlying value supporting the dress code was modesty. Showing bare skin, whether on the arms or the legs, was immodest and therefore not allowed in a religious building.

Toward Cultural Understanding

The examples are endless, but the educational meaning of these stories is clear. In order for students to become competent, caring global citizens, we need to provide opportunities for them to become less culture-bound. To be culture-bound is to define situations from the perspective of the norms of our own culture, assuming that our ways of interaction are universal.

The simplistic view of cross-cultural communication holds that if people from radically different cultural backgrounds interact, cultural understanding

Notes
① 蟋蟀
② 蟋蟀发出的短而尖的叫声
③ （通常为大型的）管弦乐队

will automatically result. This is not true, unless other knowledge has been introduced before the encounters occur. In-depth study of divergent[④] cultures, with a focus on pattern detecting, is a good place to begin with students.

A Study of Cultures

For the past seven years, two colleagues and I at Champlain Valley Union High School, in Hinesburg, Vermont, have been teaching a Comparative Cultures course. Collaboration and experimentation have been integral parts of developing and teaching the course; this year we expanded our collaborative efforts to full team teaching. We convinced the administration to remove a wall between our classrooms and decorated our new double room with art and artifacts from cultures around the world. We replaced old furniture with small, round tables.

Cognizant[⑤] of recent research on "dimensions of learning," we focus on keeping students engaged in the highly motivating processes of: inquiry, oral discourse, problem solving, decision making, and writing composition as they pursue a deeper understanding of diverse cultures. Mindful of research on how the brain works, we know we must provide meaningful tasks for students. We enable students to learn from each other in cooperative groups, as well as in total class discussion. They discuss and analyze case studies, stories, and other materials. They identify communication patterns, articulate role behavior of individuals and families at work and play, and perceive the connections between these and the culture's world view.

As students learn to use the anthropologists' conceptual tools, they become cultural pattern detectors. Given a wide variety of primary and secondary resources, print and multi-media, students draw inferences about social roles and norms, use of time and space, attitudes toward ethnicity, special linguistic features, and more. Not all activities are intellectually "heavy," however. We experiment with brush painting, mask-making, paper-cutting, and we sample the food and play games from around the world.

Other aspects of team teaching are of equal importance to us as educators. We believe that our human world needs more empathy, compassion, and commitment to collaborative efforts, if we are to survive. Team teaching provides students with models of cooperation and collaboration in action. It

Notes
④ 分歧的
⑤ 已知道的

shows them that standards for respect extend beyond the one-teacher image, and that it is good for one person to build on another's ideas.

Throughout the course one of our main goals, though, is to teach students to become cultural pattern detectors. While studying China, for example, we ask students to ponder such questions as: What belief systems, ethical traditions, values, and patterns of thinking are embedded in the Chinese culture, forming their unique view of the world? What cultural patterns of expectations, rules, and regulations pervade their daily interactions? What cultural clues give people guidance about how to behave in varied situations?

These are some of the big questions that can provide a framework for guiding investigations of smaller sets of actions. A belief system embedded in the Chinese culture can be seen in the following example. In China, it is considered an insult to tip shopkeepers. The deeply rooted Confucian ethical principles of accepting and carrying out one's duties (based on one's status) prescribe avoidance of special treatment as an individual. Being singled out as a shopkeeper and receiving a reward for doing one's duty is a source of public shame. Chinese culture gives special meaning to the word *shame*, which is a primary method of social control. Being publicly shamed causes one to "lose face," to be exposed as unethical. It is to be avoided at all costs.

In teaching our students about diverse cultures, such as Japan, Russia and the Middle East, we stress that cultural relativism, in the sense of accepting as "good" any and all cultural patterns, is to be avoided. Female infanticide[6] is not "good." Neither is any form of slavery. Students need to grapple with ethical questions concerning humaneness as they expand their understanding of what it means to be human. Sources that can guide the thinking process include the *United Nations Declaration of Universal Human Rights* and publications by such organizations as Cultural Survival, American Ethnological Society, and Minority Rights Group.

To keep pace with our students, who over the years have grown more sophisticated as cultural pattern detectors, we've had to make substantial changes in our materials and methods. We are using Edward T. Hall's conceptions of cultural patterns as common culturally determined ways of behaving in a given society. One critical learning activity focuses on Hall's notions regarding cultural context.

Notes
⑥ 杀婴

As a final project for their in-depth studies, our current students select a culture of their choice not studies in the course and apply their pattern-detecting skills to investigate it. Sorting through information, they search for significant patterns of world view, communication, social roles and norms, work and leisure, and ethnicity. In the process, they find evidence of continuity amidst change and current problems and conflicts. After organizing their findings, they present them to the class. They then share their learning with the whole school in a one-day International Festival.

Freedom from Boundaries

Cultural understanding does not automatically result when people from different environment interact. To communicate effectively and build bridges of appreciation and mutual respect, individuals must bring to the encounters cultural pattern-detecting skills. Teachers can do much to help their students break the bonds of their culture-boundness, enabling them to become multicultural people. Perhaps they, or the students who come after them, can even shed their ethnocentric biases entirely and appreciate and value honored, culturally distinct differences.

(Adapted from "Education for Cross-Cultural Communication" by Martha Ozturk)

Questions

1. What was the lesson that the author learned from his experience of shopping at Liulichang?
2. According to the author, what is the initial step for teachers and educationists to take to improve students' intercultural awareness?
3. What was the process that the author and his colleagues took in order to improve the students' intercultural communication competence?
4. How can cultural understanding be achieved?

Passage 3 ▶ Multicultural Education: Learning Styles in a Multicultural Classroom

Multicultural education is an idea, an approach to school reform, and a movement for equity, social justice, and democracy. Specialists within multicultural education emphasize different components and cultural groups. However, a significant degree of consensus exists within the field regarding its major principles, concepts, and goals. A major goal of multicultural education is to restructure schools so that all students acquire the knowledge, attitudes, and skills needed to function in an ethnically and racially diverse nation and world. Multicultural education seeks to ensure educational equity for members of diverse racial, ethnic, cultural, and socioeconomic groups, and to facilitate their participation as critical and reflective[①] citizens in an inclusive[②] national civic culture.

Multicultural education tries to provide students with educational experiences that enable them to maintain commitments to their community cultures as well as acquire the knowledge, skills, and cultural capital needed to function in the national civic culture and community. The acquisition of such experience, nevertheless, is based on the successful operation of multicultural classrooms which usually involves much challenge because students from different cultural backgrounds tend to bring with them culturally-bounded learning styles. Therefore, the following paragraphs illustrate the different learning styles from three different perspectives, namely cognitive styles, relational styles, and motivation styles to provide a glimpse of multicultural classrooms.

Cognitive Styles

Field independence versus field sensitivity. Cultures differ in the manner in which they perceive their environment. These perceptual differences are reflected in the classroom by an emphasis on either the field (the whole concept) or the parts of the field. Field-sensitive individuals have a more comfortably focus on impersonal, abstract aspects of stimuli[③] in the environment. They prefer to work with others, seek guidance from the teacher, and receive rewards based on group relations. In contrast, field-independent students prefer to work independently, are task oriented, and prefer rewards

Notes
① 思考的
② 包括许多或全部的
③ 刺激物（stimulus 的复数形式）

based on individual competition. Low-context, highly industrialized, individualistic societies such as the United States are predominantly field independent, whereas high-context, traditional, collectivistic societies like Mexico and Japan are field sensitive.

Cooperation versus competition. Cultures vary in the degree to which they stress cooperation or competition. African Americans, Asian and Pacific Rim④ Americans, Filipino⑤ Americans, Hispanic⑥ Americans, and Hawaiian Americans tend to raise their children cooperatively. This emphasis is manifested in the classroom by students working together on class assignments. For example, in Hawaiian families, children are brought up by multiple caretakers, particularly older siblings. This behavior extends to the classroom and is evidenced by high rates of peer interaction, frequently offering help to peers or requesting assistance from them. Teachers who understand which of their students respond to cooperative learning and which students prefer more competitive situations can provide classroom opportunities to accommodate both.

Trial and error versus "watch then do." In the United States, students learn how to solve problems and reach conclusions by trial and error. They practice over and over, expecting and accepting mistakes, until they become skilled. In other cultures, individuals are expected to continue to watch how something is done as many times and as long as necessary until they feel they can do it. This "watch then do" approach is characteristic of many Asian students.

Tolerance versus intolerance for ambiguity. Some cultures are open-minded about contradictions, differences, and uncertainty. Other cultures prefer a structured, predictable environment. In the United States, there is a low tolerance for ambiguity in the classroom. As such, the school day is high structured and students move from subject to subject based on the clock. We saw, through the example of the Mexican classroom, that not all cultures function in this way. What is taught in the classroom is also affected by the level of tolerance or intolerance for ambiguity. For example, American culture emphasizes right/wrong, correct/incorrect, yes/no answers, whereas cultures in India have a high tolerance for ambiguity and never regard truth in absolute terms.

Notes
④ 环太平洋地区
⑤ 菲律宾的
⑥ 拉丁美洲的

Relational Styles

Direct versus indirect communication. Culture influences the degree to which communication in the classroom is direct or indirect. Generally speaking, Americans value frank and blunt[⑦] ways of expression. However, this level of openness is often shunned[⑧] by Asian Americans, particularly first-generation immigrants, because such behavior often causes both the sender and the receiver to lose face. In addition, these cultures view such directness as a lack of intelligence. A Chinese proverb states, "Loud thunder brings little rain."

Formal versus informal communication. Values regarding formality and informality can cause serious communication problems. These difficulties are extended to the classroom. For example, in Egypt, Turkey, and Iran, teacher/student relationships are extremely formal and respectful. An Egyptian proverb exemplifies this formal respect: "Whoever teaches me a letter, I should become a slave to him forever." In cultures that value formal communication, students are expected to rise when the teacher enters the room, and teachers are addressed with their appropriate titles and last names, or referred to honorably as "teacher." In Taiwan, China, for example, students rise when the teacher enters the room, and in chorus they say, "Good morning, teacher." They remain standing until the teacher gives them permission to be seated. When students hand papers to teachers, they use both hands, avoid looking them in the eye and bow.

Topic-centered communication versus topic-associating communication. The manner in which students examine and study a topic is influenced by culture. European and American students tend to be topic centered in their approach. That is, their accounts are focused on a single topic or closely related topics, are ordered in a linear fashion, and lead to a resolution. For example, a topic-centered approach might include a rendition of a day at camp when candles were made. It would begin with the selection of different colored wax and progress to heating the wax, dipping the string in the wax, and finally cooling the wax in water to set the candle. In contrast, African American students often use a topic-associating approach. Their accounts often present a series of episodes linked to some person or theme. These links are implicit in the account and are generally left unstated. For instance, a topic-associating

Notes
⑦ 坦诚的，直率的
⑧ 回避

approach might include a rendition of the purchase of a new coat. Their story might include the following information: it was summer when the coat was purchased, the plastic bag had to be kept away from baby sister, cousin began to cry because he wanted to wear the new coat outside to play, and mother was not at home that day. When instructors are not familiar with the topic-associating approach, they may not allow the student to finish his or her thought.

Dependent versus independent learning. Culture influences the degree to which students rely on the support, help, and opinions of their teachers. Compared to European and American students, many but not all Hispanic, Filipino, and Southeast Asian students tend to be more interested in obtaining their teachers' direction and feedback. When teachers are aware of this issue, they can develop an effective support strategy in the classroom for students who show little initiative or independence.

Participatory versus passive learning. In some cultures, students are taught to participate actively in the learning process by asking questions and engaging in discussion. In other cultures, the teacher holds all the information and disseminates it to the students, who passively listen and take notes. Many Hispanic, Asian, and Pacific Rim cultures expect their students to learn by listening, watching (observing), and imitating. However, critical thinking, judgmental questioning, and active initiation of discussion are expected from students in the American school system.

Reflectivity versus impulsivity[9]. Culture influences how long students think about a question before arriving at a conclusion. In the United States, students are taught to make quick responses to questions. Impulsive students respond rapidly to tasks; they are the first ones to raise their hands to answer the teacher's question and the first ones to complete a test. In other cultures, students are reflective and seek answers slowly. In cultures that emphasize reflectivity, if one guesses or errs[10], it is an admission of not having taken enough to find the correct answer. This can result in a painful loss of face. Asian and Native Americans are examples of students who are taught to examine all sides of an issue and all possible implications before answering.

Aural[11], **Visual, and Verbal Learners**. Culture influences whether students are primarily aural, visual, or verbal learners. For example, Native Americans tend to be visual learners. Native Indian students frequently and effectively use coding with imagery or remember and understand words and concepts. They use mental images to remember or understand, rather than using word association. In contrast, many students, including African American, Haitian[12] Americans and Hmong[13] Americans tend to be aural learners. Haitians usually have a highly developed auditory ability as evidenced by the oral traditions and rote learning methods. Because the Hmong do not have a written language, they have highly developed aural skills. When the classroom contains aural, visual, and verbal learners, a multisensory approach to teaching is often effective.

Energetic learning versus calm learning. Cultural background influences whether students function better in highly active and animated classrooms or calm and placid[14] environments. African American students are used to more stimulation than is usually found in school. Many African American children are exposed to high-energy, fast-paced home environments, where there is simultaneous variable stimulation (e.g., televisions and music playing simultaneously and people talking and moving in and about the home freely). Hence, low-energy, monolithic[15] environments (as seen in many traditional school environments) are less stimulating.

Motivation Styles

Intrinsic versus extrinsic motivation. Motivation is a primary concern for the multicultural teacher who must employ a variety of motivational techniques that coincide with the students' cultural backgrounds. In addition, some students are motivated intrinsically to succeed, whereas others are motivated extrinsically. European and American students generally are motivated to learn for intrinsic reasons. For example, many European and American students desire to succeed academically so that they can secure a good position and earn a great deal of money. In contrast, Asian students are often motivated extrinsically. Asian children are often found to be motivated extrinsically by their parents and impress their relatives.

Learning on demand versus learning what is relevant or interesting. All cultures require children to learn many things whether they want to or not. However, some cultures emphasize learning what is useful and interesting rather than learning information for the sake of learning. The Japanese culture and Chinese culture, for example, require that all students memorize information such as dates, complex sequences, and lengthy formulas in mathematics, science, and social studies. Each student is also required to learn how to play a musical instrument, regardless of his or her musical ability, and instruction often begins in first grade. In contrast, the Hispanic and Native American cultures stress the importance of learning what is relevant and useful. Native American students prefer to learn information that is personally interesting to them. Therefore, interest is a key factor in their learning. When these students are not interested in a subject, they do not control their attention and orient themselves to learning an uninteresting task.

In conclusion, in light of the different examples, it should be clear that multicultural educators have a complex matrix of learning styles to attend to in a multicultural classroom. It may be impossible to accommodate all of these learning styles simultaneously. However, when teachers are aware of these various learning styles, they can better choose which pedagogical methods are most appropriate for their particular classroom.

(Adapted from "Multicultural Education — History, the Dimensions of Multicultural Education, Evidence of the Effectiveness of Multicultural Education" by James A. Banks & John Ambrosio, and from "Communication Between Cultures" by L. A. Samovar, R. E. Porter & L. A. Stefani)

Questions

1. What is the goal of multicultural education?
2. How do the learning styles of students from different cultural backgrounds differ from each other?
3. Could you summarize the learning styles of Western and non-Western students?
4. What do you think is the most crucial difference between Western and non-Western students? Why?

PART ❸ Exercises

Section A▶ Culture Quiz

Watch the two video clips of Professor Deardorff, a famous expert of intercultural communication studies from Duke University, and fill in the blanks with the words or phrases you hear.

Some of the ways that students can develop their intercultural competence include through (1)_____, of actually putting themselves into the situations in the classroom or (2)_____ where they actually have to interact with those from other cultures. This may mean pushing one's (3)_____ and that's really an important piece to do to move outside one's (4)_____ to really experience interactions with those who are different. And to start with that, it also starts with understanding one's own (5)_____ and then beginning to understand others.

So there are a number of reasons why intercultural competence is important and it depends on the (6)_____ and who you are asking. It can range from the importance of needing this for employability to (7)_____. For me personally, it can be summed up by the call from (8)_____, who said we must learn to live together as brothers or perish together as fools. So it's not something (9)_____, we must learn to live together through the center intercultural competence in order to address the problems that face us as (10)_____.

Section B▶ Group Discussion

An American teacher is teaching English in a Chinese university. Recently she has complained to you about some students who seemed to have offended her in the following occasions. Could you try your best to explain to the teacher what the misunderstandings were and tell her how she should respond to these students? You may discuss with your partner for the answers.

Occasion 1

I have a number of students with excellent academic reports. They are very attentive in class and always listen carefully to my instructions. They have very good scores for the tests as well. But they refuse to answer my questions voluntarily in the class and seem to be very embarrassed when I pick them up. This is very strange.

Occasion 2

I once had a conversation with parents of the students in my class. I explained to the parents of one student that their child needs to spend more time working on his homework. The parents kept nodding and saying "yes" as I explained my reasons. However, there doesn't seem to be any follow-up on the parents' part. I feel very disappointed.

Section C Intercultural Practice

Please decide which of the following situations are more likely to happen in Asian schools and which are more likely to happen in Western schools. And try to explain why there are differences between Asian schools and Western schools.

Typical Situations in Asian Schools	Typical Situations in Western Schools

1. Professor encourages students to ask questions in class.
2. Professor paces voice and volume to sound welcoming and friendly.
3. Professor realizes some students will chat, use social media, eat, and maybe even nap.
4. Professor believes students learn best from the voice of experience and by working through cases or problems alone.
5. Professor delivers information and students work quietly on their own.
6. Professor is expected to know answers and maintain status.
7. Professor will be gentle if a student gives wrong information saying something like,

"Good guess."

8. Professor may not know all the answers and is comfortable with this.

9. Professor relies on homework and tests to see if students are learning.

10. Professor will tell students that they are wrong.

11. Professor is formal in class but quite friendly with students outside of class.

12. Professor organizes experiences so students can learn by doing (often in groups).

13. Professor is informal in class but quite formal in meetings outside of class.

14. Professor tries to make the material simple enough that almost everyone can get it.

15. Professor shares slides, pauses for note-taking, and generally tries to set a pace that all can follow.

16. Professor may sit on a table, drink coffee, and dress casually.

17. Professors stand to lecture.

18. Professor may be quieter or louder depending on style and materials. Making students comfortable may not be a goal.

19. Professor makes the material challenging so everyone must work hard and even the strongest students are challenged.

20. Professor keeps students hopping and it is up to them to keep up or not.

21. Professor would like to be seen as an open-minded, easy-going, and knowledgeable facilitator.

22. Professor thinks students should have strong grasp of basic facts and memorize key items.

23. Professor indicates that education is a luxury to be valued and students had better work hard.

24. Professor expects some students to comment on class procedures and complain about marks.

25. Professor is happy to see students in office hours.

26. Professor thinks when a student asks for advice they should be non-judgmental and provide resources.

27. Professor would like to be seen as a confident, authoritative, expert, lecturer and guide.

28. Professor thinks when students seek advice they must share their wisdom and experience and guide the student to a good path.

29. Professor thinks memorization of key data is not as needed as an understanding of problem-solving skills for the area of study.

30. Professor indicates that education is a right for every citizen and he/she will help everyone.

Section D Case Studies

Case 1

Without a Group

Lee comes from China and is beginning his first semester at Conestoga College. Serge is from Russia. Both spent a lot of time and money studying English back home so they could pass the entry requirements for English skills, but neither has much experience listening to or speaking English. Neither studied how education occurs in Canada.

During the first 3 weeks of class discussions Lee has not contributed anything. He is uncomfortable whenever the teacher stops lecturing and opens conversations.

Serge has been giving answers in class. He speaks quite forcefully sometimes giving 5–7 sentences. The teacher just responds briefly. Once, the teacher actually said, "Let's hear from someone else now."

In the third week, the teacher assigns a group report and asks the class to get into groups of 3–4. Within minutes students have sorted themselves out and Lee and Serge are without a group.

Questions

1. What do you think has caused Lee's quietness?
2. What do you think has prompted Serge's involvement?
3. What pre-verbal, non-verbal, verbal, and post-verbal mismatches are likely to occur throughout this encounter?
4. Did either party reach the desired outcome for themselves or for the class? Why or why not?

Case 2

In this video, a group of students from different cultural backgrounds are attending a class together. Watch the video and try to discuss the following questions.

Questions

1. What are the cultural conflicts that have been manifested in this video?
2. What are the reasons do you think that have caused the conflicts?
3. Can you give some suggestions for managing a classroom with students from different cultural backgrounds?

PART ❹   Additional Reading

Chinese Students Adjust to American Education: When East Meets West, Differences Abound

Lili Gu recalls his initial trepidation (不安) at the flood of white faces in his Massachusetts high school when he came to America for 10th grade. There was the hulking football player who noticed that Gu was lost one day and said — here, Gu speaks in a guttural (喉音的) half-grunt — "Hey, you want to go to the gym? And I'm like, dude, is this guy going to rob me?" He struggled with English, too. The writing skills he arrived with, he says, would be at home in the fourth grade. But an English-as-second-language program made him comfortable after a semester. Then his formidable Chinese secondary education kicked in.

Gu says he breezed through high school, especially math, sprinting through the curriculum and into Harvard night school for advanced calculus. The easy ride ended at BU, however. If Chinese high schools are more rigorous than those in the United States, the reverse is true for universities, Gu says. Back home, "as soon as you step in the front door of a great university, it's almost like your motivation ends, because in China, GPA is not a big deal. Whether I'm a C student or D student, as long as I have that diploma, I'm awesome. If I wanted to graduate from BU with Cs, I'd probably have had a very good time."

The differences between Chinese and U.S. education matter in both countries, as students from the People's Republic surge onto American campuses. That includes BU, where Chinese students are the largest foreign contingent (about 2,000 undergraduates and grad students, 6 percent of the total) in an increasingly international student body.

A new book by Jin Li, *Cultural Foundations of Learning: East and West*, argues that the two systems fundamentally diverge: our Western education aims to convey knowledge to comprehend the world, while Chinese schools stress learning as a means to develop inner virtue. *New York Times* columnist David Brooks celebrates this supposed Chinese approach, crediting it with "awesome motivation explosions." But Li is middle-aged — she grew up during China's 1966–1976 Cultural Revolution — and Chinese students here think her take is outdated. "Seriously? Cultivate virtues? I don't think so," says Yijing Lu

Instead, the students interviewed by BU Today characterize the differences like this: Chinese high schoolers bust butt (努力工作) compared with their American counterparts in pursuit of the Holy Grail of university admission. "Failing the college entrance exam means the end of the world," says Lu, whose high school forbade dating because it was a distraction from studying. Once at a university, however, many students in China goof off (吊 儿郎当；不认真工作), either from burnout in high school or simply because they can. "Some of my friends who study in Chinese colleges tell me that they play the video game *Dota* (魔兽) day and night," says Lu.

There's also truth, according to our interviewees, to the claim that Chinese education stresses the memorization of facts, while BU, and by extension other US schools, demands more on self-education outside the classroom and practical applications of the class knowledge.

Ying "Phoebe" Zhang says the Chinese have a phrase, "learning machines," for students who pursue top grades out of obedience to demanding parents, and they're not universally celebrated. "For my parents, they don't want me to be a learning machine," she says. "You have to learn how to be a human, how to get along well with others." At the same time, says Haisu Yuan, China is bathed in traditional Confucian respect for learning, and "nerds are welcomed."

Students say adjusting to the American system was not a huge problem. For them, the main hurdles were the language barrier and occasional xenophobia (恐外症). Zhang, who came to Massachusetts starting with 11th grade at a private school, remembers her roommate announcing up front "that she hates Chinese." The roommate talked on the phone late into the night, unconcerned that she was disturbing Zhang's sleep. Overcoming her initial hesitation about speaking up — a reserve many Chinese feel when they're just learning English, Zhang says — "I had a really huge fight with her." The roommate backed down, eventually becoming Zhang's best friend.

Like Gu, Zhang found high school "super-easy." She was one of a trio of Chinese women who got their own special class in advanced calculus. She also got some behind-the-back teasing for her smarts. "At first, it really bothered me. Later, I was like, 'OK, just let them say what they want. This is my life. I have the control.'"

At BU, her biggest adjustment was learning to take outside-the-classroom initiative for learning, rather than being a passive receptacle of professorial lectures. "Professors are there to help you out when you have problems," she says. "They can give you some hint. But you have to think outside of class."

Gu and Yuan say American universities' emphasis on student responsibility for learning is an advantage. "U.S. schools are more about helping students to explore their individual power," says Yuan, while in China, "study is only for exams, so all you have to do is just practice, instead of learning."

Gu was vice president of the BU Chinese Students and Scholars Association (BUCSSA), which tries to ease the adjustment for Chinese newcomers. Its efforts begin before students set foot on campus, he says. The BUCSSA uses social media to reach newcomers the summer before they arrive, offering to arrange airport pickups and transportation to dorms. Its Chinese-language orientation each fall offers guidance on things from cultural issues to keeping track of visas and other travel documents; last year, it invited a local banker to discuss (in English) how to open a bank account.

While columnist Brooks lauds Confucian learning-cum-virtue, Zhang says the question of which system is better depends most on a student's personality. "I would say half of the Chinese students here are happy about their life," she estimates, with the other half "desperate" to return home after graduation. "They feel kind of hopeless. They really want a sense of hope, they want to feel welcome, with people they can talk to."

"If you have a high level of self-regulation, it's definitely a good idea for you to come to America," says Zhang. "You can enjoy your life, and meanwhile you are actually learning something that's useful when you are in society later on. But if you just want to get rid of the whole pile of work in China and enjoy a vacation…forget about it. Your life will be much easier there."

(Adapted from "Chinese Students Adjust to American Education: When East Meets West, Differences Abound" by Rich Barlow)

Questions

1. Could you summarize the major concerns of Chinese students studying in American universities?
2. What suggestions would you like to give to the students who are going to study abroad?

Intercultural Communication for Business

The work ethic is cultural norm that places a positive moral value on doing a good job and is based on a belief that work has intrinsic value for its own sake.

— Cherrington et al.

Live together like brothers and do business like strangers.

—Arabian proverb

PART ❶ Warm Up

Read the following story and answer the questions below it.

Rebecca works with United Technologies, a Chicago-based company. She is talking on the phone to Abhinav, the Indian manager of one of United Technologies vendors for customer service outsourcing.

Rebecca: We really need to get all of the customer service representatives trained on our new process in the next two weeks. Can you get this done?

Abhinav: That timeline is pretty aggressive. Do you think it's possible?

Rebecca: I think it will require some creativity and hard work, but I think we can get it done with two or three days to spare.

Abhinav: OK.

Rebecca: Now that our business is settled, how is everything else?

Abhinav: All's well, although the heavy monsoons this year are causing a lot of delays getting around the city.

Two weeks later…

Abhinav: We've pulled all of our resources and I'm happy to say that 60% of the customer service representatives are now trained in the new process. The remaining 40% will complete the training in the next two weeks.

Rebecca: Only 60%? I thought we agreed that they all would be trained by now!

Abhinav: Yes. The monsoon is now over so the rest of the training should go quickly.

Rebecca: This training is critical to our results. Please get it done as soon as possible.

Abhinav: I am certain that it will be done in the next two weeks.

1. Did Abhinav agree to the initial timeline requested by Rebecca?
2. What might Rebecca be thinking about Abhinav?
3. What might Abhinav be thinking about Rebecca?
4. Do you think this incident will affect their future interactions? Why or why not?

PART ❷ Readings

Passage ▶ 1 Cross-Cultural Solutions for International Business

Globalization, the expansion of intercontinental[①] trade, technological advances and the increase in the number of companies dealing on the international stage have brought about a dramatic change in the frequency, context and means by which people from different cultural backgrounds interact.

Cross-cultural solutions to international business demands are increasingly being viewed as a valid and necessary method in enhancing communication and interaction in and between companies, between companies and customers and between colleagues. Cross-cultural consultancies are involved in aiding companies to find solutions to the challenges cross-cultural differences carry.

International and national businesses are ultimately the result of people. As with incompatible software, if people are running on different cultural coding, problems can occur. Cross-cultural consultancies therefore concentrate their efforts on interpersonal communication.

Different cultures and cultural backgrounds between a highly diverse staff base tend to bring about obstacles, challenges and difficulties. Coss-cultural differences manifest in general areas such as in behaviour, etiquette, norms, values, expressions, group mechanics and nonverbal communication. These cross-cultural differences then follow on through to high level areas such as management styles, corporate culture, marketing, HR and PR.

Notes
① 洲与洲之间的

In order to overcome potential pitfalls[2], specialist attention is required in the form of a cross-cultural consultant. As one would approach a doctor for a medical diagnosis[3] or an accountant to examine finances, cross-cultural consultants offer the expertise, experience and know-how to diagnose problems and provide solutions to interpersonal cultural differences.

Within companies there are many facets in which cultural differences manifest. Some key areas which cross-cultural consultants deal with include, but are not exclusive to, the following:

Cross-Cultural HR: HR covers a wide range of business critical areas that need cross-cultural analysis. Consultants may offer advice on a number of areas including recruitment, relocation, international assignments, staff retention[4] and training programmes.

Cross-Cultural Team-Building: in order to have a well functioning business unit within a company, communication is critical. Cross-cultural consultants will provide tools and methods to promote staff integration, reduce cross-cultural conflicts and build team spirit. This is essentially done through highlighting differences and building on strengths to ensure they are used positively.

Cross-Cultural Synergy: international mergers, acquisitions and joint-ventures require people from different cultural backgrounds to harmonise in order to succeed. Cross-cultural consultants counsel on group mechanics, communication styles, norms, values and integration processes.

Cross-Cultural Awareness Training: working with colicagues, customers or clients from different cultural backgrounds, with different religions, values and etiquettes can occasionally lead to problems. Cross-cultural awareness training is usually a generic introduction into a culture, country, region or religion. The aim is to equip the trainee with the adequate knowledge to deal comfortably with people from different cultures, avoiding misunderstandings and mistakes.

Cross-Cultural Training for Expatriate Relocation: staff that travel overseas need to understand the cultural basics of the host country or region. Knowledge of the country's history, culture, laws, traditions, business practices and social etiquettes all help to minimise the impact of culture shock and hence smooth their transition overseas.

Notes
② 意想不到的危险或困难
③ 诊断
④ 保留

Cross-Cultural Negotiations: equipped with their knowledge of the two or more cultures that can be meeting around the negotiation table, a cross-cultural consultant advises on areas such as negotiation strategies, styles, planning, closure and etiquette in order to increase the chance of a successful outcome, free from misunderstandings, suspicions[5] and general cross-cultural communication breakdown.

Cross-Cultural PR Consultancy: brand image, public relations and advertising are all areas companies must be careful of when moving out of the national context. Tastes and values change dramatically from continent to continent. It is crucial to understand whether the brand name, image or advertising campaign is culturally applicable in the target country. Cross-cultural consultants examine words, images, pictures, colors and symbols to ensure they fit well with the target culture.

Cross-Cultural Language Training: Language training is an area where little investment is made by companies, but where the business advantages are great. Linguistic knowledge goes a long way in bridging cultural gaps and smoothing lines of communication. Cross-cultural consultancies provide language training to business staff, moulding[6] their learning to the business environment in which they work.

In conclusion, clearly the role and expertise of cross-cultural communication consultants is important for today's international business. The potential pitfalls cross-cultural differences present to companies are extensive. In essence a cross-cultural consultant's primary objective is integration. This integration, between colleagues, clients and customers is crucial for business success. Equipped with experience, knowledge and above all objectivity, a cross-cultural consultant creates bridges of understanding and opens lines of communication.

(Adapted from "Cross-Cultural Solutions for International Business" by Neil Payne)

Notes
⑤ 猜疑
⑥ 塑造或影响某人

1. Why do you think intercultural communication has been expanding rapidly in the world today?
2. What are the forms of intercultural communication that can be involved in international business?
3. In the eight areas mentioned in the text, which one do you think should be prioritized for intercultural communication consultancy? Why?

Passage 2 ▶ Ten Strategies for Success Abroad

Working across cultures requires a diverse skill set and a different approach of business in general. When bridging with foreign cultures, certain strategies are crucial to international business success. Here are ten strategies for interacting with people from different cultures.

Learn About the Business Beforehand.

This general business strategy becomes increasingly important when dealing with businesses across cultures. Get on their website, check out their promotional[①] material. Get a feel for the atmosphere, attitude, and angle that the business has. Many cultural factors are passed down from the societal level to businesses. However, each organization will have its own culture, personality, and way of doing things.

Notes
① 增进的

Observe.

As your mind is processing a lot of information in new environments, your observation skills may be flooded or unfocused when working across cultures. Keeping your observation skills engaged and alert to elements will help you do business. Notice how people act, dress, and treat each other. If you come from a culture that emphasizes verbal communication, make a point of looking for messages that are conveyed without being said. Being able to read a situation will greatly improve your ability to have a successful meeting.

Ask Questions.

Many people don't want to reveal how little they know about other cultures, so they don't ask questions. Ultimately, they may limit their ability to work in other cultures. Questions can show you are interested in your colleagues' cultures. Such interest and consideration will help you build your relationship, which is especially important if your culture has a reputation for trying to culturally dominate others (e.g. the U.S.). Demonstrate that you are working to create synergy[2] between your cultures with questions. In doing so, you create room for the mistakes you may make; people are more willing to look past cultural blunders[3] if they know you are trying to learn about the culture you are working with.

Stay Aware of Yourself.

Some people feel like they have somewhat of an out-of-body experience when in cross-cultural situations because they are focused on everything new outside of themselves. There can be so much going on around you that you forget to focus on yourself as well. Take advantage of down time[4] (and make time for it) so you can get in touch with your body and feelings. What's your gut feeling? Where is it coming from? This process can help you feel more grounded and secure in your experience abroad.

Notes
[2] 协同作用
[3] （愚蠢的或粗心的）错误
[4] 停工时间

Allow for More Time.

Working across cultures takes more time. Communication may be slowed and logistics may be different. You may be working with a culture with a different concept of time altogether. Expect most things to take longer than they would when dealing with a business from your same culture or country. Also give yourself more time to process all the information before making decisions.

Look for Individual Differences.

Overviews of cultures are meant to be guidelines only. Individuals may have values and behaviors that vary greatly from those of their native culture. Many people make the mistake of trying to fit people they are working with into cultural molds, while often they don't fit. People's values and behaviors are influenced in part by their culture, but also by their background, experiences, and personality. Be careful not to attribute too much of what you observe to a cultural difference.

Find the Humor.

Humor heals and helps you through difficult situations. Travel can be stressful, as can be new environments and change in general. Such stress can limit both your flexibility and your ability to handle cross-cultural situations. Combat stress with humor. Be able to step away (at least mentally) from situations and find the humor in them.

Learn to Tolerate Uncertainty.

This is an essential skill, and one that can be extremely difficult for people from some cultures where directness and exactness are valued (e.g. Germany, the U.S.). There will be a great deal of unknowns when you do business across cultures. Definitive, concrete answers may not always be given, especially if you are working with a culture with a high tolerance for uncertainty. Focus on what you can determine and try to let go of minor details that are unclear. (Similarly, if you come from a culture that doesn't place a high value on exactness and are working with someone from a culture that does, try to provide clarification and details when possible.)

Go Early.

If your meeting is face-to-face and you'll be traveling abroad, go a few days before your scheduled meeting. Give yourself time to adjust; you will have to deal with physical adjustments (jet lag, different foods) as well as a number of cultural adjustments. These changes can be overwhelming[5] and should be spread out to make them manageable. Give yourself time to adjust physically and then your mind will be better prepared to make cultural adjustments that are essential for success.

Build Your Intercultural Skills.

When working with people from different cultures, you need a solid understanding of the norms of that culture. You also need communication skills and business strategies that can be applied across cultures. The items listed above reflect some of the necessary skills for intercultural work in general. However, individuals need to further their intercultural competence based on their own situations and needs.

To determine what skills you need to develop, reflect on past intercultural experiences (for people with limited experience abroad, think of experiences working and interacting with people and groups different from you). When do you become uncomfortable, rigid, or shut down? What mistakes have you made in the past? Commit yourself to continually developing the skills that will help you in similar situations in the future.

View your experiences with different cultures as a trajectory, rather than a string of individual experiences. Link the different experiences you have and you can link the personal development and learning that comes with them.

(Adapted from "Ten Strategies for Success Abroad" by Kate Berardo)

Questions

1. How can asking questions help people in intercultural business occasions?
2. Why do you think it is important to learn to tolerate uncertainty when doing business in cross-cultural contexts?
3. Are there any other skills that you can suggest for international businesspersons?

Passage 3 ▶ Intercultural Communication in the Global Workplace

With the increased globalization of workplace settings across most industries, today's managers need a more precise understanding of intercultural communication in an effective management strategy. It is important that managers proactively[①] engage in communication skills assessment and make necessary adjustments in order to address the current needs of today's increasingly diverse workforce. When assessing intercultural communication, it is important to have a plan in place and keep these points

Notes
① 预先

in mind:

Know Your Team:

While getting to know as many cultures as possible is a noble endeavor, in reality managers are strapped[2] for time like everyone else. If your functional outsourcing group is diverse, or you have recently hired a new group of employees, or your company is reaching out to more overseas investors, then you have a great opportunity to develop more effective intercultural communication skills that will be most applicable to your team as an integrated part of your diversity training initiatives.

A consultant certified with significant coursework in intercultural communication can lead a productive discussion group with managers to explain key elements of intercultural communication that can improve employee/client relations and contribute positively to work productivity. Understanding topics such as: international nuances[3] regarding the concept of personal space in business interactions; the connotation of punctuality in meetings and planned interactions; and different perspectives on maintaining eye contact, can help managers create a more conducive and welcoming work environment.

Among the more technical skills a manager with intercultural communications can offer his or her team is an understanding of the fundamental focus of various cultures on the written word (content) versus the manner and delivery of those words (context). Understanding some of these basic principles can provide strong insight into selecting the most effective methods of communicating with and managing your business interactions. Even if you do not get it right all the time, employees and business partners will appreciate your willingness to meet him or her on common ground, and this motivates all parts of your team to work cohesively reaching for the highest potential.

Do Your Homework:

Just as in any group, there are differences among individuals, and understanding general distinctions within a cultural group is important. Do your homework without singling out individuals. One major area is religious beliefs. After honing④ their own intercultural skills, managers should be able to lead effective training sessions to explain nuances of several cultural beliefs that may impact work related situations. If a team member's religion requires prayer during the day, remember not to schedule essential meetings at that time; this will convey the message that the team member is important. Allowing flexibility around holy days when possible builds an appreciation of management. Gender balance in groups is important to those who discourage single women from being alone with men. Creating a workplace where there is not just a tolerance of difference, but an embracing of it can go a long way to productive business relationships.

Other cultural considerations that could be helped with greater intercultural communication skills include: gender differences, generational differences, and socio-economic differences. Of course, these components overlap other cultural considerations, so a manager with intercultural training from a reputable university also generally has an ongoing network of peers who can act as mentors as intercultural communication challenges arise.

Notes
④ 磨砺
⑤ 有责任的

The Platinum Rule:

Most current diversity training programs include the tenet that it is no longer good enough to use the golden rule when dealing with other people in the way you want to be treated. In today's global workplaces, it is incumbent⑤ upon managers to step up their managerial skills to what has been coined as the "Platinum Rule." Managers who want to remain competitive in the global marketplace and who want to lead effective teams working with heightened synergy know that they must exercise an understanding of how the other person wants to be treated in a business setting. Taking the time to get to know the individuals in your group requires a more robust set of managerial soft skills, and effective ways to implement those skills without making an individual feel singled out.

In conclusion, an effective intercultural communication program should provide a diverse set of skills that are easily applicable to a manager's unique situation and setting. Skilled professionals who are leaders in their field can provide not only the knowledge, but the personal experience to make the concepts come alive. Instruction with self-assessment allows the individual to tailor the program toward the skills necessary for personal success. Having access to an ongoing library of materials and peer networking for long term success and development are also key features of a quality intercultural communication program for managers striving for excellence in today's increasingly diverse global workplace.

(Adapted from "Intercultural Communication in the Global Workplace" by the University Alliance of the University of Notre Dame for online certificate programs of Mendoza College of Business)

Questions

1. What should a manager do in order to know his or her team? What should he or she know?
2. What is the "homework" that a manager should do for employees from various cultural backgrounds?
3. What is the "platinum rule?"
4. Could you compare the strategies offered in Passage 2 and Passage 3, and find out the differences between them?

PART ❸ Exercises

Section A▸ Culture Quiz

Guess and choose the most appropriate answer to each of the following questions according to your knowledge about different cultures.

1. Which of these is the most important on business cards in Germany?
   A. Age.   B. Qualifications.   C. Years at current company.
2. Business cards are always reciprocated in the U.S.
   A. True.   B. False.
3. You should accept cards in Japan with _____.
   A. both hands   B. the left hand   C. the right hand

4. Exchanging business cards is very ceremonious in the U.K.

   A. True.   B. False.

5. Which of these should you not do to a Koreanman's business card?

   A. Write on it.   B. Comment on it.   C. Look at it.

6. What color would you suggest wrapping a gift in for a client in India?

   A. Green.   B. White.   C. Black.

7. Why would you not give a Brazilian a knife for a gift?

   A. It represents the cutting off of a head.

   B. It represents the cutting off of a relationship.

   C. It represents the desire to marry the recipient's daughter.

8. In Japan, gifts are considered bribes.

   A. True.   B. False.

9. In Belgium, when should gifts be given to a host?

   A. After the meal.   B. Before the meal.   C. During the meal.

10. When giving or receiving a gift in China, you should do so using _____.

    A. both hands   B. the right hand   C. the left hand

11. Which of these gifts is the most appropriate for a Saudi business associate?

    A. Gold watch.   B. Silver pen.   C. Silk tie.

12. Reciprocal gifts in South Korea should always be _____.

    A. more expensive   B. of equal worth   C. cheaper

13. When meeting with the French in a business environment, which of these should
    be avoided?

    A. Personal questions.   B. Eye contact.   C. Formal demeanor.

14. Which of these statements is true?

    A. German decision-making can be very slow.

    B. Germans take a casual approach to punctuality.

    C. Germans expect humor in a business context.

15. Upon being met at the office of a potential Indonesian client, you are met with very
    personal questions about your job, education and salary. Why?

    A. Because these questions are just part of the getting-to-know-you process.

    B. Because these questions are meant to establish your rank.

    C. Because these questions are thought to be of importance in your own country, so
       they are being asked out of politeness.

Section B▶ Group Discussion

Try to find out the negotiating style of Asian and the Western countries under the following topics. You may refer to the Internet or library for reference and discuss with your partner for the answers.

Topics	Asian Countries	Western Countries
1) Negotiating goal		
2) Negotiating attitude		
3) Personal style		
4) Communication		
5) Sensitivity to time		
6) Emotionalism		
7) Form of agreement		
8) Building an agreement		
9) Team organization		
10) Risk-taking		

Section C▶ Intercultural Practice

Choose the best response in the following business occasions.

1. During negotiations in Japan, you try to confirm a point by asking, "Do you not want this added to the agreement?" You are answered with a "yes," so you keep it within the agreement. At a later date you find the Japanese are upset that this was added to the agreement. Why?

   A. The Japanese's positive answer to negative questions actually meant "no."

   B. "Yes" can sometimes mean "maybe." In this case the Japanese team wanted to think about it, so "yes" meant "let us think about it and check with us at the next meeting."

   C. The Japanese assumed you knew they did not want it to form part of the agreement and answered "yes."

2. Your company has been negotiating with a company in Argentina for 3 months. The next round of negotiations is set to be the final meeting, with all sides aiming for an agreement. The negotiator who had been dealing with Argentina is ill and cannot travel. A replacement is briefed and sent to clinch the deal. He returns empty-handed. Why?

   A. The Argentine company was simply offended because they assumed your company was not taking the corporate relationship seriously by sending in a new negotiator.

   B. In Argentina, personal relationships are valued more than corporate ones. The negotiations failed because the new negotiator was unknown.

   C. In Argentina, the belief is that if illness gets in the way of business, it is a bad omen.

3. During intense negotiations, the Russian negotiation team keeps pressing you on a particular point you absolutely cannot budge on. You have politely indicated your position to no avail. They are insistent. Which of these options would be the most advisable?

   A. Keep politely insisting you that are unable to satisfy their demand. The Russians will eventually understand.

   B. Drag your negotiation team out of the room dramatically. The Russians will then appreciate that concessions on this point are unlikely.

   C. Concede slightly. The Russians will then feel that they have gained some sort of concession and move on.

4. At the end of your negotiations with a Chinese firm, the negotiation team suddenly demands that you drop your prices or they may have to pull out of any agreement. What should you do?

   A. Stand firm. They are merely trying to test your resolve and gain some last-minute concessions.

   B. Ask for time to speak to your superiors.

   C. Agree. The Chinese would not do so unless there is a good reason due to the need to save "face."

5. In Hong Kong, you and your counterpart share a cup of tea. During the negotiations, you notice that he keeps moving his cup either closer to you or further away. Why?

   A. Because this is a method used in *feng shui* to gain positive energy.

   B. Because this represents how far away/close you are to agreement.

   C. Because this indicates nervousness and should be capitalized upon.

Section D▷ Case Studies

Case 1

A U.S. golfing equipment manufacturer decided to explore the possibility of entering the Japanese market. They arranged a meeting with a major Japanese firm to discuss a joint venture. Three representatives of each firm met up in San Francisco. Following the initial introductions the men sat down at opposite sides of the table. After offering their Japanese guests a drink the U.S. representatives proceeded to take off their jackets and roll up their sleeves as a sign of "let's get down to business." The meeting was unsuccessful and the joint venture never took place.

Question

What cultural faux pas (失礼) did the Americans make?

Case 2

Jonathan Manning has been chosen to set up a branch of his engineering consulting firm in Seoul, Korea. Although the six engineering consultants who would eventually be transferred there are British, Jonathan is interested in hiring locals as support staff. He is particularly keen to hire an accountant. He is offering a great salary with excellent working conditions. He gets some names put forward through contacts he has in Seoul. After meeting with them he is surprised to find all of them turn down his offer. All preferred to stay with their current employers.

Question

Why did all the Korean contacts prefer to stay with their current employers?

Case 3

Watch a video clip about cultural differences, in business and answer the following questions.

Questions

1. Why do you think Valerie Hoeks experienced culture shocks during her stay in China?
2. What are the suggestions given by Valerie Hoeks for dealing with culture shocks?
3. What are the other suggestions that you would like to give to foreigners doing business in China?

PART ❹   Additional Reading

Culture in Advertising

Culture is a little like dropping an Alka-seltzer (泡腾片) *into a glass — you don't see it, but somehow it does something.*

— Hans Magnus Enzensberger

Culture affects everything we do. This applies to all areas of human life from personal relationships to conducting business abroad.

When interacting within our native cultures, culture acts as a framework of understanding. However, when interacting with different cultures, this framework no longer applies due to cross-cultural differences.

Cross-cultural awareness aims to help minimise the negative impact of cross-cultural differences through building common frameworks for people from different cultures to interact within. In business, cross-cultural solutions are applied in areas such as HR, team building, foreign trade, negotiations and website design.

Cross-cultural solutions are also critical to effective cross-cultural advertising. Services and products are usually designed and marketed at a domestic audience. When a product is then marketed at an international audience the same domestic advertising campaign abroad will in most cases be ineffective.

The essence of successful advertising is convincing people that a product is meant for them. By purchasing it, they will receive some benefit, whether it be lifestyle, status, convenience or financial. However, when an advertising campaign is taken abroad different values and perceptions as to what enhances status or gives convenience exist. These differences make the original advertising campaign defunct.

It is therefore critical to any cross-cultural advertising campaign that an understanding of a particular culture is acquired. By way of highlighting areas of cross-cultural differences in advertising a few examples shall be examined.

Language in Advertising

It may seem somewhat obvious to state that language is key to effective cross-cultural advertising. However, the fact that companies persistently fail to check linguistic implications of company or product names and slogans demonstrates that such issues are not being properly addressed.

The advertising world is littered with examples of linguistic advertising blunders. Of the more comical was Ford's introduction of the "Pinto" in Brazil. After seeing sales fail, they soon realised that this was due to the fact that Brazilians did not want to be seen driving a car meaning "tiny male genitals."

Language must also be analysed for its cultural suitability. For example, the slogan employed by the computer games manufacturer, EA Sports, "Challenge Everything" raises grumbles of disapproval in religious or hierarchical societies where harmonious relationships are maintained through the values of respect and non-confrontation.

It is imperative therefore that language be examined carefully in any international or cross-cultural advertising campaign

Communication Style in Advertising

Understanding the way in which other cultures communicate allows the advertising campaign to speak to the potential customer in a way they understand and appreciate.

For example, communication styles can be explicit or implicit. An explicit communicator (e.g. U.S.) assumes the listener is unaware of background information or related issues to the topic of discussion and therefore provides it themselves. Implicit communicators (e.g. Japan) assume the listener is well informed on the subject and minimises information relayed on the premise that the listener will understand from implication. An explicit communicator would find an implicit communication style vague, whereas an implicit communicator would find an explicit communication style exaggerated.

Colors, Numbers and Images in Advertising

Even the simplest and most taken for granted aspects of advertising need to be inspected under a cross-cultural microscope. Colors, numbers, symbols and images do not all translate well across cultures.

In some cultures there are lucky colors, such as red in China and unlucky colors, such as black in Japan. Some colors have certain significance; green is considered a special color in Islam and some colors have tribal associations in parts of Africa.

Many hotels in the U.S. or U.K. do not have a room 13 or a 13th floor. Similarly, Nippon Airways in Japan do not have the seat numbers 4 or 9. If there are numbers with negative connotations abroad, presenting or packaging products in those numbers when advertising should be avoided.

Images are also culturally sensitive. Whereas it is common to see pictures of women in bikinis on advertising posters on the streets of London, such images would cause outrage in the Middle East.

Cultural Values in Advertising

When advertising abroad, the cultural values underpinning the society must be analysed carefully. Is there a religion that is practised by the majority of the people? Is the society collectivist or individualist? Is it family orientated? Is it hierarchical? Is there a dominant political or economic ideology? All of these will impact an advertising campaign if left unexamined.

For example, advertising that focuses on individual success, independence and stressing the word "I" would be received negatively in countries where teamwork is considered a positive quality. Rebelliousness or lack of respect for authority should always be avoided in family orientated or hierarchical societies.

By way of conclusion, we can see that the principles of advertising run through to cross-cultural advertising too. That is, know your market, what is attractive to them and what their aspirations are. Cross-cultural advertising is simply about using common sense and analysing how the different elements of an advertising campaign are impacted by culture and modifying them to best speak to the target audience.

(Adapted from "Culture in Advertising" produced by Kwintessential Ltd.)

Questions

1. In what ways do you think culture may influence advertisements?
2. Could you find some examples of successful/unsuccessful intercultural advertisements?

Intercultural Communication for Cyberspace

I am not an Athenian or a Greek, but a citizen of the world.

— Socrates

When in Rome, do as the Romans do.

— English proverb

While life can not adapt to us, we should adapt to life.

— Anonymous

If you know the enemy and know yourself, you need not fear the result of a hundred battles. If you know yourself but not the enemy, for every victory gained you will also suffer a defeat. If you know neither the enemy nor yourself, you will succumb in every battle.

— Sun Tzu

PART ❶ Warm Up

Imagine you are submitting a piece of written work via e-mail to your academic professor to read and you want to ask him to provide feedback. What would happen if your e-mail was not properly written? Now please discuss with your partners which of the following requests are appropriate and which are inappropriate by putting a tick (√) accordingly and then explain why.

Request	Appropriate	Inappropriate	Not sure
1. Teacher, I need your advice.			
2. I do need to get your feedback on this.			
3. I'm looking forward to any feedback you can provide.			
4. Please notify me, hopefully before the weekend is over, on what I should do.			
5. If possible, please review the draft and reply to me through e-mail tonight or early next morning.			
6. I want to know the results of my final exam, so please let me know as soon as possible.			
7. Here is my essay. Please help me to check it.			
8. Please help me.			

PART ❷ Readings

Passage 1 ▶ Living Language

Recently, I worked in China for two months, teaching English to university students who plan to come to Australia to study. It was my first time in China for a few years and I noticed that I was having trouble understanding the students when they spoke Chinese among themselves. My Chinese used to be pretty good. When I was working in China in the 1980s, I scored the highest level possible in the HSK[①], the Chinese equivalent of TOEFL. Why couldn't I understand a lot of what they said now? Of course, some of this was because my Chinese has gone rusty[②]. As the old saying goes, if you don't use it, you lose it—practice is so important in language learning. Some of it might also have been that my ears had not adjusted to the local accent. But after a while, I became more and more convinced that the main reason why I was having trouble was language shift. The Chinese of today simply isn't the same language that I learnt in the 1970s and 1980s.

All languages evolve over time. A classic example in English is the word gay. In my parents' time, gay meant "cheerful" or "happy." Then about fifty years ago, it shifted its meaning and came to mean homosexual. Both English and Chinese have changed a lot in the past thirty years. Sometimes I even have trouble understanding my own teenage daughters at home. The English that they speak is not exactly the same as the English I spoke when I was their age.

One of the biggest reasons for language shift in recent years is technology. When I was young, a *window* was something you opened to let in some fresh air and a *mouse* was a small animal. Now they both refer to computers. Social networking (itself a redefined concept) has also given us new words such as tweeting[③]. When I first learnt Chinese, *wang* meant a "net" as in the game of tennis, but now it usually refers to the internet. We now have words such as *wangzhan* (website) and *wangba* (internet café). Popular websites have become new words in themselves. Young people in China today often use words like QQ and Alibaba. These words would have made no sense

Notes
① 汉语水平考试
② 生疏
③ （社交网络）推特

at all just a few years ago. In fact, the expression *zaixian* (online) had a completely different meaning years ago, when it was used in a very negative way in phrases such as *zaisiwangxianshang* (on the verge of death) (在死亡线上).

The use of mobile phones and texting④ has also led to many changes in language. I don't think the word *shouji* (mobile phone) would have made any sense to me at all when I was first learning Chinese back in high school. And in English, the word text used to be a noun, but now it is often used as a verb! Many abbreviations used in text messages have now moved into the spoken language. I now hear teenagers in Australia using words like lol⑤ (laugh out loud) and omg⑥ (oh my God). Some abbreviations have even been made shorter again — for example, OK is now often shortened to simply k.

Acronyms⑦ are not new to the English language, but they seem to be becoming more common all the time. Popular ones at the moment include yolo (you only live once), bff (best friends forever — sometimes said as biffle) and bae (before anyone else — meaning girlfriend or boyfriend). And older people get their revenge by skiing⑧ (spending the kids' inheritance)

Australians have always loved to shorten words. Even back in my youth, people used words such as arvo⑨ (afternoon). Now we have totes⑩ (totally), selfie⑪ (a photo of yourself) and halfie⑫ (a person of mixed Asian and European blood). Youngsters greet each other with sup⑬ (what's up?). One expression that my daughters use a lot is shipping⑭, as in "I ship this person and that person" (I think there might be/wish there would be a relation between these two people). Australians also love to use sarcasm⑮. When a young Australian describes something as lame or sick, they are actually saying they like it or approve of it!

Perhaps the most famous piece of slang of all time is cool. First made popular in America in the 1960s, it has persisted, where other slang words come and go with fads and fashions⑯. In the 1990s, cool even made its way into Chinese slang, with many young people using the character *ku* to write it, which originally had a very negative meaning.

Since the "opening-up" policy, China as a society has changed greatly and this has also led to changes in the language. The expression *langxin* (wolf heart) used to refer to brutal and unscrupulous⑰ people; now a best-selling

Notes
④ 发短信
⑤ ［俚语］大声笑
⑥ 我的天啊
⑦ 首字母缩略词
⑧ 花孩子们的遗产
⑨ ［俚语］下午
⑩ ［俚语］完全
⑪ ［俚语］自拍
⑫ ［俚语］混血儿
⑬ ［俚语］你好吗
⑭ ［俚语］希望两个名人有关系
⑮ 反语
⑯ 时尚潮流
⑰ 无道德原则的

book is suggesting that *langxinguanli* (wolf management⑱) is the way to succeed in the business world. Students use English acronyms such as GDP and WTO, as if they are Chinese expressions. The influence of English has also led to words that really make no sense in Chinese, such as ma'te (market) and mini (small).

When I first visited China, parking lots were called *tingchechang*, but now the Hong Kong expression *boche* seems to be more popular. Back in the 1980s, people referred to their husbands and wives as *airen* (lovers), but now old expressions such as *laopo* and *laogong* have made a comeback.

Language is always changing. I am sure the readers will be able to think of many more examples of new words and words whose meaning has changed in recent years. Maybe some day soon we will need to use google translate just to communicate between the generations.

(Adapted from "Living Language" by Craig Keating)

Notes
⑱ 狼心管理

Questions

1. Why was the author having trouble understanding Chinese although he scored high level in the HSK?
2. What is one of the biggest reasons for language shift? Could you please cite some examples?

Passage 2 ▶ The Impact of New Media on Intercultural Communication

The history of human communication began with the oral or spoken tradition. Through the course of history, the dissemination① of messages progressed from simply the oral tradition, to script, print, wired electronics, wireless electronics and finally digital communication. The greatest change in message dissemination in recent history occurred with the introduction of computers and the Internet in the early 1990s. Since then, this drastic change of communication medium has significantly affected humans' perception of the media, the usage of time and space, and the reachability and control of the media.

Notes
① 传播

In the present age of digital communication, time has been compressed by reducing the distance between different points in space, and the sense of space has led people to feel that local, national, and global space becomes obsolete[2]. In addition, the reachability of digital media can now extend to all people, instead of a limited audience. This is significant because without the confinement[3] of time and space, the control of message production and dissemination is no longer a privilege possessed only by church, state, and government, but instead, equally shared by all individuals. All these innovations in digital media, or so-called new media, have changed and continue to change the way we think, act, and live.

New media has brought human society to a highly interconnected and complex level, but at the same time, it challenges the very existence of human communication in the traditional sense. New media not only influences the form and content of information/messages, but it also affects how people understand each other in the process of human communication, especially for those from different cultural or ethnic groups.

Intrinsically, the new culture hatched from new media creates a continuity gap between traditions and innovations within a culture. Before the emergence of new media, traditions and innovations in human society co-existed in a dynamically synchronized[4] way, but the speed and impact of the new media resulted in the inability of traditional values to keep pace with the new cultural values produced by new media. This cultural gap has caused difficulty in understanding or communication between generations and among people in the same culture.

New media also extrinsically breeds communication gaps between different cultural and ethnic groups. The fragmented nature of new media has switched traditional cultural grammar, cultural themes, or cultural maps to a new pattern, resulting in the loss of traditional cultural logic. The rearrangement or restructuring of cultural patterns, or world view, demands that members of a culture realign[5] their communication behaviors within their own community, and to learn a new way of interaction with people from differing cultures. New media fosters a new culture in human society, in which the degree of ambiguity and uncertainty has been reshuffled and has reached its highest point, especially in the process of intercultural communication.

Notes
[2] 过时的
[3] 限制
[4] 同步的
[5] 重组

How to readjust to this new situation and smoothly achieve the goal of mutual understanding for people from different cultural groups in this chaotic stage of cultural change becomes a great challenge for the practical need of interaction in daily life and research in the scholarly community. It is under this circumstance that we see more and more scholars are becoming involved in the investigation of the relationship between new media and intercultural communication.

1. National / Ethnic Culture and New Media

As Weick pointed out, in the international electronic exchange culture plays a significant role in affecting the process and outcome of the interaction. In other words, culture as a communication context may dictate the use of media. Chen found that three cultural factors, namely thinking patterns, expression styles, and cultural context, are the three prominent cultural factors that influence how people behave in electronic media, and the three factors are the manifestation of cultural values. Based on the distinction of low-context culture and high-context culture categorized by Hall proposed possible communication differences for members in the two groups in the process of electronic interaction (see Table 1):

Table 1. Differences between Low- and High-Context Cultures in
E-communication

	LCC	HCC
Meaning display	explicit	implicit
Value orientation	individual	group
Personal relationship	transitory	permanent
Action base	procedure	personal
Logic	linear	spiral
Message learning time	short	long
Verbal interaction	direct	indirect
Nonverbal style	individualistic	contextual
Idea presentation	logic	feelings
Message style	detailed	simple
Credibility source	authority	communication source

It is assumed that cultural values will influence the social networking process in new media. Hall's low-context and high context cultures and Hofstede's individualism and collectivism dimensions of cultural values are two of the most common models used in the study of the relationship between culture and media. For example, cultural value orientations affect a user's attitude when using new media. Their study demonstrates that although the motives for using social media are similar for students, those in high-context, collectivistic cultures, such as Korean college students, show more emphasis on attaining social support from existing social relationships, while those in low-context, individualistic cultures, such as American college students, tend to show more interest in seeking entertainment rather than social relationships. Moreover, compared to high context, collectivistic cultures in the process of new media interaction, people in low-context, individualistic cultures tend to emphasize individual achievements and self-promotion to extend their social relations network, though the orientation may trade privacy in the network.

2. New Media and Intercultural Interaction

New media, especially social media such as Facebook, blogs, MySpace, YouTube, Twitter, and the iPhone, have enabled people from every corner of the world to represent themselves in a particular way and stay connected in cyberspace. It is obvious that the flexibility of information presented and shared in the new media will directly affect, either positively or negatively, the development of intercultural relationships in the virtual community through the creation of a network of personal connection.

Moreover, in foreign language and study abroad contexts, the use of blogging not only shows a positive effect on the development of intercultural relationships, but also increases the degree of participants' intercultural communication competence. In addition to intercultural relationships on a personal level, social media also helps to establish international business relationships. Nevertheless, new media may also produce a negative impact on intercultural communication. For example, revealing too much personal information in blogs, especially negative information about one's friends, employer, and others, tends to jeopardize[6] or cause problems in establishing constructive human relationships intraculturally and interculturally.

Notes

[6] 使（某事物）受到伤害、损失或破坏

Notes
⑦ 四海一家

Finally, it is argued that computer-mediated communication can promote and develop virtual cosmopolitanism⑦ and virtual third cultures. The authors indicated that through the construction of third culture space, a new, hybrid culture is created, in which interactants from differing cultures are able to gather cultural and social information, build online communities, and form intercultural relationships.

Because new media enables individuals across the globe to exchange messages for the purpose of understanding people from different cultures, it has become popular for sojourners or immigrants to use new media to communicate with their friends, classmates, and relatives or family members in both their native and host country in their learning process or daily life. As shown in Chen's study, the longer immigrants reside in the host country, the more they communicate with the host nationals via new media, but the frequency of surfing their original country's websites is decreasing. Also the use of new media shows a significant impact on the process of immigrants' intercultural adaptation. In other words, the social interaction conducted through new media by immigrants proves to be a critical element that can determine whether they can successfully adjust to the host country.

In addition, Sawyer and Chen investigated how international students use social media and how it affects their intercultural adaptation. The authors found that social media provides an environment for international students to connect with people in both their home and host countries, which in turn helps them strengthen personal relationships and fosters a sense of belonging to the host culture. The use of new media obviously helps international students cope with cultural barriers in the process of intercultural adaptation. The study also found that, due to the influence of culture shock, sojourners tend to rely more on social media in the initial stage of arriving in the host country, to keep connected with those people they know in their home country in order to gain a sense of comfort in the new environment. As time moves on, the use of social media was switched to interacting with the host nationals to help them better integrate into the new culture.

New media not only provides a space in which people of different cultures can freely express their opinions and establish relationships, but may also challenge the existence of human communication in intracultural and intercultural contexts because of its specific characteristics that are significantly dissimilar to traditional media.

(Adapted from "Impact of New Media on Intercultural Communication" by Guo-Ming Chen)

Questions

1. Could you please explain what new media is and what social media is by giving some examples respectively?
2. What do you think is the relationship between ethnic culture and new media?
3. How does social media affect intercultural communication in cyberspace?

Passage 3 ▶ The Role of Social Media in Intercultural Learning

Notes

① 美国热门图片分享社区（目前是继Facebook、Twitter后又一个受世界瞩目的网站）

② 一款支持iOS、Windows Phone、Android 平台的移动应用，允许用户在任何环境下抓拍下自己的生活记忆

③ 一款非常受欢迎的跨平台应用程序，用于智能手机之间的通讯

A day without access to new technologies, online tools and digital media is something many of us cannot imagine. We use Facebook to keep in touch with friends, Twitter to follow the news, Pintrest① to organize our hobbies, Instagram② to share our pictures, Whatsapp③ and many other instant messaging systems to chat with friends, family and colleagues all over the world. A recent survey commissioned by Nokia shows that on average, people check their phones at least 150 times per day. This made us wonder: How does the online interaction between people affect the development of intercultural competences and what are its implications for issues such as support for social adaptation?

Jason Lee, Ph.D. of AFS Malaysia (Yayasan Antarabudaya Malaysia) and associates conducted a study at the National Institute of Education in Singapore in 2012 aiming to find these answers as they relate to AFS exchange students. The study entitled *Uncovering the Use of Facebook during the Exchange Program* was conducted in order to find out whether Facebook has a role in coping with exchange-experience related stress, and in building social identity and intercultural competences.

Notes
④ 动态更新
⑤ 参与

The research methodology was based on examining status updates④ of Malaysian secondary school students going on an exchange in the U.S., as well as interventions⑤ such as interviews and questionnaires before and after their year abroad. A total of 917 status updates and 3,246 corresponding comments made between January and July 2009 were analyzed. The material was classified into categories and traced over the U curve cultural adaptation model in four critical periods: pre-departure, arrival, in-exchange and return.

Even though there is no hard evidence that the use of new media creates cultural awareness, it is possible to look at certain impacts of Facebook through the so-called "ABCs" of intercultural adjustment — its affective, behavioral, and cognitive aspects.

The affective side of intercultural learning can be seen as a result of undergoing a series of stress-provoking life changes, according to Colleen Ward in *The Psychology of Culture Shock*. In this case, stress does not need to be only a negative event, but also a learning opportunity and a motivating factor to do better in the future.

This study showed that, in the affective, or feeling, domain, Facebook is used as a resource for coping with stress: Sojourners express emotions in status updates and in return receive support from their friends. Facebook statuses are a way to acknowledge the stressor and sometimes even add humor to the situation. This is perceived as an indirect way to seek help, while lightening the problem and minimizing vulnerability with humor.

Although friends' comments can have a negative effect too, the positive responses from them often serve the purpose of support and can inspire further reflection about the issue. They also make the participants learn something about themselves — their own identity and culture, and this increased self-awareness is one of the Educational Goals of AFS exchange programs. Facebook status updates are also used for coping with the changed environment and keeping in touch with people from home. Such statuses may lead to "group mediated cognition," a situation where the opinion of an individual is influenced by the thinking of peers involved in the same activity.

In exchange, social media is also a space where participants often compare their performance, or cultural adaptation process, with their peers. This comparison can affect them in two different ways: An "upward comparison" with somebody who is perceived to be coping with the challenges better than them can result in increased motivation to progress. Or, in a "downward comparison," exchange students can look for self-validation[6] and ways to cope with adaptation-related stress by realizing that they are not the only ones in such a situation.

The behavioral aspect of intercultural learning, on the other hand, as it is defined in this study, describes the need to acquire culture-specific knowledge and social skills in order to successfully adapt in an environment, according to this study. While the use of Facebook can be analyzed in the affective and cognitive domains, the behavioral aspect was not included in this analysis as participants did not use this social medium frequently enough in search for culture-specific information.

In this study, the cognitive aspect is based on Tajfel's social identity theory, which describes the formation of one's identity as a dynamic process involving intergroup relations and acculturation strategies. In the cognitive domain, Facebook status updates and interaction can play a role in acculturation (see *Cultural Adaptation Models for Friends of AFS* for more information). While also building their virtual identities, students gain awareness and take critical stands on their own culture while maintaining their identity.

This research shows that through their postings, sojourners were able to identify aspects of their own culture which are particularly important to them, or which may have previously been invisible to them. At the same time, Facebook status updates are also used as a means to seek or build relationships with the host community.

This research shows that social media can be used by exchange students to externalize[7] feelings and as a resource of social support throughout the learning experience. While this kind of online communication does not replace in-person contacts and support structures that AFS has for its participants, it can be a useful supplement. And, it is important to bear in mind that excessive Internet use is one of the dysfunctional[8] coping strategies, which was confirmed by the results of the Impact of Living Abroad study.

Some other reports also indicate that social media can also be useful in the post-exchange communication and dealing with the so-called reverse culture

Notes

[6] 自我验证
[7] 外在
[8] 不正常的

shock⁹ or re-entry problems. In the upcoming issues of this news magazine we will look at the post-exchange challenges sojourners face and how digital tools can help in overcoming them.

(Adapted from "The Role of Social Media in Intercultural Learning" by Milena Miladinovic)

Notes

⑨ 逆向文化冲击

Questions

1. What are upward comparison and downward comparison respectively based on the passage?
2. Do you think online communication can replace in-person contacts ? Why or why not?
3. What do you think are the advantages and disadvantages of using social media?

PART ❸ Exercises

Section A Culture Quiz

Listen to the recording and supply the missing words in the blanks.

The job market is more (1)_____ than ever for millions of workers around the world. In America, one reason right now is the slow (2)_____ in job growth after the recession.

But other reasons involve changes in the needs of the American and (3)_____ economies. In big developing economies like India and China, high (4)_____ rates mean workers often move from job to job.

These days, many job (5) _____ go online to connect with employers. Job candidates want to show they have a lot to (6)_____. But in many cases they simply apply for a job (7)_____ and list their work experience. Instead, they should describe the (8)_____ and abilities they could bring to an organization.

That is the advice of Steve Langerud, director of professional opportunities at DePauw

University in Indiana. He advises students on (9)_____ planning and often talks about workplace issues in the media.

He says social media sites are (10)_____ when they show the abilities of job candidates and not just their job title and experience.

Section B ▶ Group Discussion

Read the following information and then discuss the questions below with your group members.

Social networking sites like Facebook and Twitter, audio and video download sites such as iTunes, YouTube, and Netflix, search browsers like Google, wi-fi technology, mobile communication devices, and teleconferencing systems such as Skype demonstrate their indispensability across wide-ranging modernities.

The Internet and social media are pervasive and transformative forces in contemporary China. Nearly half of China's 1.3 billion citizens use the Internet, and tens of millions use Sina Weibo, a platform similar to Twitter or Facebook, and QZone are popular social networking sites as well. Now Wechat has become another major form of social media in China.

1. What do you think are the purposes of social media in our life? How involved are you with social media sites?
2. Do you feel satisfied or fulfilled after using social media? Why or why not?
3. Is there anything else you would like to say about social media and intercultural communication?

Section C ▶ Intercultural Practice

Based on the video clip, write an essay entitled "The Impact of Virtual Network on Intercultural Communication" with no less than 150 words. The following information is just for your reference.

Positive influence:
- new learning opportunities such as free online courses
- improving language skills such as listening and reading
- cultural interaction to know more about belief, thoughts, tradition, etc.

- easy access to limitless number of E-books and to purchasing what people like

- …

Negative influence:

- terrorist groups and extremist propaganda

- vulnerability of personal information like data lost and identity theft

- problems of fraud, hacker, etc.

- disconnectedness from the real world

- …

Section D▶ Case Studies

Case 1

Facebook Users

In the past few years, Facebook has risen to become the top SNS(Social Network Site) with over 40 languages, occupying the second most popular site in the world, after Google, and the first SNS. By the beginning of 2011, Facebook has attracted more than 21.31 million users across the Arabic countries. By October, 2011, Facebook has spread to more than 33.07 million Arab users.

A notable difference between the West and Arab world is that, while more than 50% of the Western Facebook users(e.g. U.S., U.K., Canada, Australia, Netherlands, Sweden, Denmark, Norway, Spain, and Ireland) are female, on the average, only about 36% of Arabic Facebook members are female. There is another significant demographic difference between the Arab world and the West regarding the age groups of Facebook users. The majority of Facebook users in the Arab world(55%) is in the range between 13 to 24 years old, and mostly are students. Facebook users in the West for the same age group represents only about 36%, and the majority of them lies in range between 25 to 60 years and older, and mostly are outside of college.

(Adapted from "The Impact of Arab Cultural Values on Online Social Networking: The Case of Facebook" by K. S. A. Omoush et al.)

Question

What are the differences between the West and the Arab world regarding the age groups of Facebook users and percentage of females engaged in SNSs? Why?

Case 2

Hallyu

From Japan to Indonesia, a certain kind of pop culture is very hot. But it doesn't come from Hollywood—it's Hallyu (韩流), the wave of Korean pop culture that has washed over Asia. It has influenced everything from music to television.

Korea produces all types of entertainment, the most popular being music, soap operas and films. What makes Hallyu so hot in Asia? One reason is that its products are of high quality and much cheaper than western products. Another reason is that eastern cultures are similar to each other, although there are language differences.

Korean pop music, or "K-pop," ranks the first everywhere. Fans love the songs and the attractive stars. Companies like SM Entertainment, JYP Entertainment and YG Entertainment help many K-pop stars, such as Super Junior, Big Bang and Rain, to succeed. They are not only popular in Asia but also enjoy popularity in the West. In 2011, Big Bang's mini-album Tonight reached the top 10 on U.S. Tunes Top Pop Albums. When SM Entertainment took their 2010 world tour to Los Angeles, only 30 percent of the 15,000 fans were Korean. Half of the audience wasn't even Asian! Thanks to the Internet and social media, Hallyu has spread worldwide.

Questions

1. What do you think makes Hallyu popular worldwide?
2. Are you familiar with the K-pop, *Gangnam Style*? Why do you think it soared to popularity globally overnight?

PART ❹ Additional Reading

Globalization, Networking and Intercultural Communication

With the unprecedented range of globalization processes, the number of contacts across cultures has dramatically increased, resulting in an unusual phenomenal spread of new social media embracing the whole world. The present day situation is characterized by great changes in many aspects of reality. Globalization has induced mobility which has led to substantial growth of various cultural contacts, resulting in a great variety of Englishes. Social media and networking have induced a new kind of communication.

Globalization

Globalization is "a social process in which the constraints of geography on social and cultural arrangements recede, and people become increasingly aware that they are receding." But most typically, as Kluver writes, globalization is defined with reference to the different forms of interconnectedness including networks. In the author's opinion, while globalization refers to integrated economic institutions, the channels of technology help this integration. The development of communications technologies enrich the scope of trade and with electronic media any novel ideas will reach the destination within an instant.

Cowen draws attention to the fact that globalization has two sides: while it has brought effective commercial influences (for example spread of Toyotas in 151 countries; Coca-Cola in 185 countries; McDonald's all over the world, etc.), at the same time it tends to ruin cultures and their ethos (信仰). The author understands the word ethos as "a shared cultural matrix (模式) for interpretation, rather than a narrow conformity of opinion." Globalization and social media promote ethnic and cultural diversity, but on the other hand we witness cultural losses. We see that uniqueness, thereby faltering in their artistic creativity."

The global phenomenon of social media, is tightly connected with new technologies and both in turn impact intercultural communication. There are voices warning about the great serious impact of new media inducing changes to life experience, and transformations in the field of economics, cultural patterns, communication styles, etc. Furthermore, the cyberspace formed by new media allows people to generate virtual experience and reality, which effectuates the free alternation of one's gender, personality, appearance, and occupation. "The invisible cyberspace not only induces a gap between reality and virtuality, also effectuates the free alternation of one's gender, personality, appearance, and occupation."

Summing up, Chen constructs five important features of globalization:

First, globalization is a dialectically dynamic process, which is caused by the pushing and pulling between the two forces of cultural identity and cultural diversity, or between localization and universalization. Second, globalization is universally pervasive (无处不在的). It moves like air penetrating into every aspect of human society and influences the way we live, think, and behave. Third, globalization is holistically (整体上的) interconnected. It builds a huge matrix in which all components are interconnected with networks. Fourth, globalization represents a culturally hybridized (混合的) state, which allows cultural transmission via new media to take place at a very rapid rate by permeating and dissolving human boundaries. Finally, globalization increases individual power in the new media society, which pluralizes the world by recognizing the ability and importance of individual components.

"With these distinct features new media pushes the trend of globalization to its highest level in human history." Movius highlights the fact that media have a central place in globalization and gives three reasons for this: 1) media corporations globalize their products; 2) global infrastructure of communication eases and promotes global information flows; 3) and global media play a key role in how we presently communicate.

Networking

Social networking as a special phenomenon has significantly impacted networked societies all over the world. A new generation has recently appeared, variously called *N Gen* (network generation), *generation D* (digital generation), *millennials* or *generation Y*, these are all those who were born in "*computer epoch.*" It could be said that the global level of networking has led to significant differences in the attitudes toward many intercultural constituents; for example, for the digital generation communication through social networks is preferable to speech, and also, the attitude toward the notion of friends is conceptualized quite differently nowadays.

The impact of social networks on various constituents of intercultural communication is underscored (强调) by many scholars. According to Shuter, "new media…are transforming communication across cultures;" electronic media have altered contemporary methods of communication. Chen argues that "with its distinctive features new media has brought human society to a highly interconnected and complex level, but at the same time, it challenges the very existence of human communication in the traditional sense." "New media not only influences the form and content of information/messages, but it also affects how people understand each other in the process of human communication." After studying a wide range of literature Chen identified three main areas of impact:

(1) the impact of national/ethnic culture on the development of new media,

(2) the impact of new media on cultural/social identity

(3) the impact of new media (especially social media) on different aspects of intercultural

interaction (e.g., intercultural relationship, intercultural dialogue, and intercultural conflict)

Summing up, we can compare the new media with the mythological two-faced **Janus**. One face gives the opportunity to talk on-line with a multitude of "friends," which the digital generation is happy to see. Social networking, by incessantly generating information due to new technologies, helps "friends" to maintain connections. But the other face of Janus threatens existence of unique minority cultures, their cultural patterns, and life experience, through the pervading globalization. Thus, the networks transform communication styles and other intercultural communication categories.

In the present research, intercultural communication is understood as integrating pragmatic, cognitive, affective, axiological (价值论的), cultural, and behavioral patterns in communication acts between two individuals belonging to different cultures (interpersonal communication) or communicative acts between groups belonging to diverse cultural contexts (intercultural communication).

Changes in Intercultural Communication

The processes of globalization and networking are tightly connected, and in turn influence intercultural communication, the vector (引导物) of which is presently directed toward the global level. The new generation that has grown up on Internet technologies has transformed the attitude to communication.

To succinctly (简明地) outline the present day cause of intercultural transformations all over the world we have to address new media which have triggered contacts of people from different cultures and caused changes from "face-to-face encounters" to instantaneous "communication with others regardless of geo-political boundaries, time, or space."

The impact of networking on intercultural communication has dramatically changed the 'standard norms' of communication, compared to the last century. Netters have acquired the so-called 'digital culture' introducing changes to linguistics, speech, the way of spending time, etc. Instead of words, netters often use abbreviations, for example, *idk* ("I don't know"); *bff* ("best friend forever"); *brb* ("be right back"); *nvm* ("never mind"); *sup* ("what's up?"); *cya* ("see ya [you] later"); *lol* ("laugh out loud"); *omg* ("oh my gosh!") *w8* ("wait"), *rolf* ("rolling on floor laughing"); *yolo* ("you only live once"), to mention just a few.

The changes in communication before social networks and presently are compared in Table 1 below.

Table 1. Comparing Intercultural Communication Before and Now

Before	Now
Face to Face (*f2f*)	Mediated(Networking)
Telephone (standard)	I-phone, cell phone
Books	E-books
Teaching	Learning
Writing	Texting / IMing
Words, collocations	Abbreviations (often)
Collaborative work (*f2f*)	Distant collaboration
Working in offices	Working at home (often)
Identity	Identity (disguised by niks)
Control of information	Information can freely move around (Chen, 2012)
Categories: Values (shared by many in a society)	New values (acquired through virtual societies, from friends living in a great variety of countries
Compliance (Reigeluth, 1996)	Initiative (Reigeluth, 1996)
Conformity (Reigeluth, 1996)	Diversity (Reigeluth, 1996)
One-way communications (Reigeluth, 1996)	Networking (Reigeluth, 1996)

The data and studies summarized in the table confirm great changes concerning intercultural communication categories. A previous study by Lebedko found that students (Chinese and Japanese) from abroad who came to Russia to study Russian language and culture used social media less during the honeymoon stage (of culture shock and/or acculturation. They gradually began using Facebook and Renren social media at the recovery stage and later they pointed out that "speaking" with friends on the nets was supporting them if students experienced cultural bumps or communication failures at the acculturation stage. Some students accepted various values (not so many) and rejected others. The study showed the impact of social media: values now are more dynamic than ever before. Shuter pronounced these tremendous changes as 'the revolution.' One can also see that the process of teaching has been transformed to learning, that gives initiative to students; e-books are preferred to books; writing has turned into Texting and

IMing; abbreviations are often preferred to words and collocations; F2F (face-to-face) collaborative work has presently changed to distant collaboration when authors who do not know personally each other, know the projects they are working on and discuss them without getting acquainted. In regard to internet "friendship," identity can be disguised when "friends" are reluctant to know their "friends" and use nicknames. The notion of intercultural communication has also changed from one way communication to networking with multiple friends. Another impact of the digital age is that previous control of information has been converted to information that can freely move around.

Conclusion

The main goal of the study was to address the processes of globalization and networking and their impact on intercultural communication. It is argued that the paradigm (范例) of communication is presently changing, for example, face to face communication is more and more often replaced with writing in social networks; and for the new generation, born in the digital era, communication through social networks is more preferable than speech. A tentative study survey was conducted with the purpose of eliciting students' attitudes to new social media. Fifty-nine students at a large Russian university were asked to answer questions concerning their communication with peers in various countries. The findings in this research include the following: 1) most students highly valued their virtual societies underscoring the help from friends in networks (Social networking is very important in contemporary world. They are inalienable (不可剥夺的) part of communication with friends). 2) Social networks are applied as an instrument in education. Students' responses showed that education is also highly valued (It helps me to learn languages, I widen my vocabulary; I have possibility to communicate with native speakers of English or Spanish; it helps me master my English and not to forget my good Spanish). 3) Communication for business to acquire (business partners, to have business relations). 4) General communication (Facebook helps me support the connection with acquaintances living abroad.). Overall, respondents reported rather strong emotions concerning their wide horizons opened to them thanks to social networking (virtual societies, education, business, general communication).

(Adapted from "Globalization, Networking and Intercultural Communication" by Maria G. Lebedko)

Questions

1. What are five important features of globalization?
2. How do globalization and networking influence intercultural communication?
3. How significant or insignificant is the networking for you? Why?

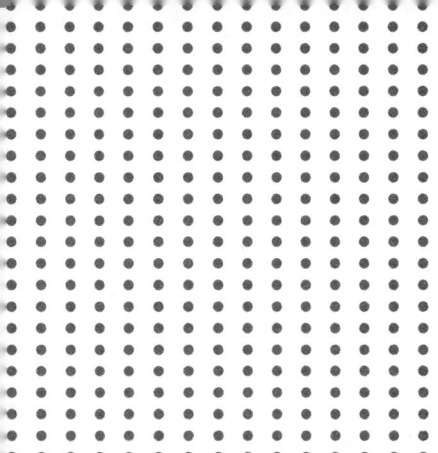

Bibliography

Allwood, J., & Schroeder, R. (2000). Intercultural Communication in a Virtual Environment. *Inter-Cultural Communication*(4), 1-15.

Asante, M. K., Newmark, E., & Blake, C. A. (1982). *Handbook of Intercultural Communication.* London: Sage Publications Inc.

Ayalew, A. T. (2012). *An Integrative Approach to Intercultural Communication in Context: Empirical Evidences from Higher Education.* Doctor of Philosophy, Justus Liebieg University, Giessen.

Bagdasaryn, N. G. (2011). Intercultural Communication in the Context of New Media.

Banks, J. A., & Ambrosio, J. (2011). Multicultural Education — History, The Dimensions of Multicultural Education, Evidence of the Effectiveness of Multicultural Education.

Barlow, R. (2013). Chinese Students Adjust to American Education: When East meets West, Differences Abound.

Berardo, K. (2007). Ten Strategies for Success Abroad. *Culturosity®Learning Center.*

Boyd, D. M., & Ellison, N. B. (2007). Social Network Sites: Definition, History, and Scholarship. *Journal of Computer-Mediated Communication*, 13(1), 210-230.

Brislin, R. W., Cushner, K., Cherrie, C., & Yong, M. (1986). *Intercultural Interactions: A Practical Guide.* Beverly Hills, CA: SAGE Publications.

Castells, M. (2000). Global Communication Via Internet: An Educational Application. In G. M. Chen & W. J. Starosta (Eds.), *Communication and Global Society* (pp. 143-157). New York: Peter Lang.

Chen, Guo-Ming., & Starosta, W. J. (1996). Intercultural Communication Competence: A synthesis. *Communication Yearbook*, 19, 353-384.

Chen, Guo-Ming., & Starosta, W. J. (2005). *Foundations of Intercultural Communication.* Lanham, MD: University Press of America.

Chen, Guo-Ming., & Starosta, W. J. (2007). *Foundations of International Communication.* Shanghai: Shanghai Foreign Language Education Press.

Chen, Guo-Ming., & Zhang, K. (2010). New Media and Cultural Identity in the Global Society. In R. Taiwo (Ed.), *Handbook of Research on Discourse Behavior and Digital Communication: Language Structures and Social Interaction.* Hershey, PA: Idea Group Inc.

Chen, Guo-Ming. (2012). The Impact of New Media on Intercultural Communication in Global Context. *China Media Research*, 8(2), 1-10.

Chen, R, Bennett, S., & Maton, K. (2008). The Adaptation of Chinese International Students to On Line Flexible Learning: Two Case Studies. *Distance Education*, 29, 307-323.

Chen, Wenli. (2009). *Internet Use and Intercultural Adaptation: A Case Study on Chinese Immi-*

grants in Singapore. Paper presented at the annual meeting of the International Communication Association, New York City.

Chen, Wenli. (2010). Internet-Usage Patterns of Immigrants in the Process of Intercultural Adaptation. *Cyberpsychology, Behavior, and Social Networking*, 13(4), 387-399.

Chung, J., & Chen, Guo-Ming. (2007). The Relationship Between Cultural Context and Electronic-Mail Usage. In M. Hinner (Ed.), *The Role of Communication in Business Transactions and Relationships* (pp. 279-292). New York: Peter Lang.

Claes, M. T. (2003). Intercultural Communication Introduced. In P. Kistler & S. Konivuori (Eds.), *From International Exchanges to Intercultural Communication: Combining Theory and Practice* (pp. Front Cover): University of Jyväskylä Press.

Dai, F., & Smith, S. L. J. (2003). *Cultures in Contrast: Mis-Communication and Misunderstanding between Chinese and North Americans.* Shanghai: Shanghai Foreign Language Education Press.

Davis, L. (2001). *Doing Culture: Cross-Cultural Communication in Action.* Beijing: Foreign Language Teaching and Research Press.

Donath, J., & Boyd, D. M. (2004). Public Displays of Connection. *BT Technology Journal*, 22(4), 71-82.

Dou, Weilin. (2005). *Intercultural Business Communication.* Beijing: Higher Education Press.

Ellison, N. B., Steinfield, C., & Lampe, C. (2007). The Benefits of Facebook "Friends": Social Capital and College Students' Use of Online Social Network Sites. *Journal of Computer-Mediated Communication*, 12, 1143-1168.

Elola, I., & Oskoz, A. (2009). Blogging: Fostering Intercultural Competence Development in Foreign Language and Study Abroad Contexts. *Foreign Language Annals*, 41(3), 454-477.

Enzensberger, H. M. (2016). Culture in Advertising. *Culture Vulture.*

Fatt, J. P. T. (1999). It's Not What You Say, It's How You Say It. *Communication World*, 16(6).

Flew, T. (2005). *New Media.* New York: Oxford University Press.

Glover, K. (1990). Do's and Taboos: Cultural Aspects of International Business. *Business America.*

Gudykunst, W. B. (1998). *Bridging Differences: Effective Intergroup Communication.* . Thousand Oaks, CA: Sage Publications Inc.

Gudykunst, W. B. (2003). *Cross-Cultural and Intercultural Communication.* Thousand Oaks, CA: Sage.

Gudykunst, W. B., Matsumoto, Y., Ting-Toomey, S., Nishida, T., Kim, K., & Heyman, S. (1996). The Influence of Cultural Individualism-Collectivism, Self-Construals, and Individual Values on Communication Styles Across Cultures. *Human Communication Research*, 22(5), 510-543.

Hall, E. T. (1976). *Beyond Culture*. New York: Doubleday.

Harvey, D. (1990). *The Condition of Postmodernity: An Enquiry Into the Origins of Cultural Change*. Oxford: Blackwell.

He, Weixiang., Jamison, J., Antoniou, P. H., & Whitman, K. (2004). *Intercultural Communication Skills*. Guangzhou: Sun Yat-Sen University Press.

Hofstede, G. (2001). *Culture's Consequences: Comparing Values, Behaviors, Institutions, and Organizations Across Nations*. Thousand Oaks, CA: Sage.

Hu, Sufen., & Yang, Y. (2015). *Intercultural Communication: Case and Analysis*. Beijing: China Agriculture Press.

Jackson, M. (2011). 10 Big Benefits of a Busy Business Blog.

Jamison, J. (2004). Globalization and Communication. In Weixiang He, J. Jamison, P. H. Antoniou & K. Whitman (Eds.), *Intercultural Communication Skills* (pp. 107-110). Guangzhou: Sun Yat-Sen University Press.

Jandt, F. E. (1995). *Intercultural Communication: An Introduction*. Thousand Oaks, CA: Sage Publications.

Jones, S. G. (Ed.). (1995). *Cybersociety: Computermediated Communication and Community*. Thousand Oaks, CA: Sage.

Keating, C. (2015). Living language. *College English*(11), 51-52, 56.

Kim, Y., Sohn, D., & Choi, S. M. (2010). Cultural Difference in Motivations for Using Social Network Sites: A Comparative Study of American and Korean College Students. *Computers in Human Behavior*, 27(1), 365-372.

Kistler, P., & Konivuori, S. (Eds.). (2003). *From International Exchanges to Intercultural Communication: Combining Theory and Practice*. Jyväskylän yliopisto: University of Jyväskylä Press.

Kohls, L. R. (2001). *Survival Kit for Overseas Living*. Yarmouth, ME: Intercultural Press.

Lebedko, M. G. (2014). Globalization, Networking and Intercultural Communication. *Intercultural Communication Studies*, XXIII(1), 28-41.

Lister, N., Dovery, J., Giddings, S., Grant, I., & Kelly, K. (2009). *New Media: A Critical Introduction*. New York: Routledge.

Liu, J. (2003). *From an EFL Learner to an ESL Leader: Reflections in a Nonnative Voice*. Speech presented at the TESOL Convention, Baltimore, Maryland.

Lustig, M. W., & Koester, J. (2007). *Intercultural Communication: Interpersonal Communication Across Cultures*. Shanghai: Shanghai Foreign Language Press.

Matsumoto, D., Hirayama, J., & Leroux, J. (2006). Psychological Skills Related to Intercultural Adjustment. In P. Wong & L. Wong (Eds.), *Handbook of Multicultural Perspectives on Stress and Coping* (pp. 387-405). New York: Kluwer Academic/Plenum Publishing.

McEwan, B., & Sobre-Denton, M. (2011). Virtual Cosmopolitanism: Constructing Third Cultures and Transmitting Social and Cultural Capital Through Social Media. *Journal of International and Intercultural Communication*, 4(4), 252-258.

Miladinovic, M. (2014). The Role of Social Media in Intercultural Learning. *AFS Intercultural Link News Magazine*, 5.

Omoush, K. S. A., Yaseen, S. G., & Alma'Aitah, M. A. (2012). The Impact of Arab Cultural Values on Online Social Networking: The Case of Facebook. *Computers in Human Behavior*, 28(6), 2387-2399.

Ozturk, M. (1991). Education for Cross-Cultural Communication. *Educational Leadership*, 49(4), 79-81.

Parks, M. R., & Floyd, K. (1996). Making Friends in Cyberspace. *Journal of Communication*, 46, 80-97.

Payne, N. (2004). Cross Cultural Solutions for International Business. *Ezine@rticles*.

Phillipson, H., & Lee, A. R. (1972). *Interpersonal Perception: A Theory and a Method of Research*. New York: Harper & Row.

Polistina, K. (2009). Cultural literacy: Understanding and Respect for the Cultural Aspects of Sustainability. In A. Stibbs (Ed.), *The Handbook for Sustainability*. Oxford: Green Books.

Qian, Hua., & Scott, C. R. (2007). Anonymity and Selfdisclosure on Weblogs. *Journal of Computer Mediated Communication*, 12(4), 1428-1451.

Rogers, E. (1995). *Diffusion of Innovations*. New York: The Free Press.

Samovar, L. A., Porter, R. E., & Stefani, L. A. (2000). *Communication Between Cultures*. Beijing: Foreign Language Teaching and Research Press & Brooks/Cole/Thomson Learning Asia.

Samovar, L. A., & Porter, R. E. (2007). *Intercultural Communication: A Reader*. Shanghai: Shanghai Foreign Language Education Press.

Sawyer, R., & Chen, Guo-Ming. (2012). The Impact of New Social Media on Intercultural Adaptation. *Intercultural Communication Studies*, 21(2), 151-169.

Sawyer, R., & Kim, Y. Y. (2001). *Becoming Intercultural: An Integrative Theory of Communication and Cross-Cultural Adaptation*. Thousand Oaks, CA: Sage Publications, Inc.

Scollon, R., & Scollon, S. W. (2000). *Intercultural Communication: A Discourse Approach*. Beijing: Foreign Language Teaching and Research Press.

Shuter, R. (2011). Introduction: New media Across Cultures — Prospect and Promise. *Journal of International and Intercultural Communication*, 4(4), 241-245.

Song, Li. (2004). *Gateway to Intercultural Communication*. Harbin: Harbin Institute of Technology

Press.

Spencer-Oatey, H. (2007). *Culturally Speaking: Managing Rapport Through Talk Across Cultures*. Shanghai: Shanghai Foreign Language Education Press.

Storti, C. (1999). *Figuring Foreigners Out: A Practical Guide*. Yarmouth, Maine: Intercultural Press Inc.

Sze, D. (2015). How Americans and Chinese Think About Happiness Differently. *The Huffington Post*.

Ting-Toomey, S. (2007). *Communicating Across Cultures*. Shanghai: Shanghai Foreign Language Education Press.

Trebbe, J. (2007). Types of Immigration, Acculturation Strategies and Media Use of Young Turks in Germany. *Communications*(3), 171-191.

Trompenaars, F., & Turner, H. (1997). *Riding the Waves of Culture: Understanding Cultural Diversity in Business*. Boston/London: Nicholas Brealey Publishing Ltd.

Tsai, H. (2006). Use of Computer Technology to Enhance Immigrant Families' Adaptation. *Journal of Nursing Scholarship*(38), 171-191.

University Alliance. (2010). Intercultural Communication in the Global Workplace. *Intercultural Management*.

Varner, I., & Beamer, L. (2006). *Intercultural Communication in the Global Workplace (3rd ed.)*. Shanghai: Shanghai Foreign Language Education Press.

Vasalou, A., Joinson, A. N., & Courvoisier, D. (2010). Cultural Differences, Experience with Social Networks and the Nature of "True Commitment" in Facebook. *International Journal of Human-Computer Studies*(68), 719-728.

Vinuales, G. (2011). *Impact of Cultural Values in Social Network Sites: The Case of Facebook*. Paper presented at the Annual conference of the Association for International and Intercultural Communication Studies, Chiapas.

Walther, J. (1992). Interpersonal Effects in Computermediated Interaction: A relational perspective. *Communication Research*(35), 79-91.

Wang, Fuxiang., & Ma, Dengge. (1999). *An Analytical Survey of Cultural Clashes*. Beijing: Petroleum Industry Publishing House.

Wang, M. M., Brislin, R. W., Wang, Weizhong., Williams, D., & Chao, J. H. (2000). *Turning Bricks into Jade*. Boston: Intercultural Press.

Wardhaugh, R., & Fuller, J. M. (2014). *An Introduction to Sociolinguistics*. Hoboken, NJ: John Wiley & Sons.

Weick, K. E. (1983). Organizational Communication: Toward a Research agenda. In L. L. Putnam

& M. E. Pacanowsky (Eds.), *Communication and Organizations: An Interpretive Approach* (pp. 13-29). Beverly Hill, CA: Sage.

Winkelman, M. (1994). Cultural Shock and Adaptation. *Journal of Counseling & Development* (73), 121-126.

Wintergerst, A., & McVeigh, J. (2011). *Tips for Teaching Culture: Practical Approaches to Intercultural Communication*. New York: Pearson Education Inc.

Xu, Lisheng. (2004a). *Intercultural Communication in English*. Shanghai: Shanghai Foreign Language Education Press.

Xu, Lisheng. (2004b). *Introducing Intercultural Communication*. Hangzhou: Zhejiang University Press.

Ye, Jiali. (2006). An Examination of Acculturative Stress, Interpersonal Social Support, and Use of Online Ethnic Social Groups Among Chinese International Students. *The Howard Journal of Communication*, 17, 1-20.

Zhang, Ailin. (2003). *Intercultural Communication*. Chongqing: Chongqing University Press.

Zhang, Ailin. (2008). *Loginto the World of Cultures — Intercultural Communication*. Chongqing: Chongqing University Press.

Zhao, Yunlong. (2002). *A Study on Intercultural Communication*. Beijing: China International Press.

郑重声明

高等教育出版社依法对本书享有专有出版权。任何未经许可的复制、销售行为均违反《中华人民共和国著作权法》，其行为人将承担相应的民事责任和行政责任；构成犯罪的，将被依法追究刑事责任。为了维护市场秩序，保护读者的合法权益，避免读者误用盗版书造成不良后果，我社将配合行政执法部门和司法机关对违法犯罪的单位和个人进行严厉打击。社会各界人士如发现上述侵权行为，希望及时举报，我社将奖励举报有功人员。

反盗版举报电话　（010）58581999　58582371
反盗版举报邮箱　dd@hep.com.cn
通信地址　北京市西城区德外大街4号　高等教育出版社法律事务部
邮政编码　100120

读者意见反馈

为收集对教材的意见建议，进一步完善教材编写并做好服务工作，读者可将对本教材的意见建议通过如下渠道反馈至我社。

咨询电话　400-810-0598
反馈邮箱　wy_dzyj@pub.hep.cn
通信地址　北京市朝阳区惠新东街4号富盛大厦1座
　　　　　高等教育出版社总编辑办公室
邮政编码　100029